IT'S AN OLD
WILD WEST CUSTOM

Other Titles in The American Customs Series

It's an Old
Wild West Custom

DUNCAN EMRICH

THE VANGUARD PRESS, INC. · NEW YORK

Manufactured in the United States of America
by H. Wolff, New York, N. Y.

To My Wife

MARION VALLAT EMRICH

and Other Western Characters

ACKNOWLEDGMENTS

Since no attempt has been made to present a bibliography, the attention of the reader may be called to the various *State Guides* which contain basic lists of books dealing with the respective states and which are, in addition, highly informative and readable. Originally prepared under the sponsorship of the United States Government, they are now published commercially for the eight states in question by Binfords and Mort Publishers, Hastings House, the Oxford University Press, and the University of New Mexico Press. The reader interested primarily in the folklore and customs of the area would do well, also, to consult the *Western Folklore Quarterly* issued by the University of California Press. A primary source for Western Americana, including the states covered in this book, its articles have maintained a high level of scholarship and readability. The publications of the several university presses in this region and of the Caxton Press of Caldwell, Idaho, as well as the specialized material issued by such organizations as the Arizona Folklore Committee and the New Mexico Folklore Society, deserve consideration as well. The annual proceedings of the Western Folklore Conference, normally held in July at the University of Denver, are of special interest to the regionalist.

I am indebted to many persons whose researches in the eight states of this book have made it largely possible: to Professor Austin E. Fife and his wife, Alta Fife, for material from their unique collection of Mormon folklore; to Professor Wayland Hand, for material from his published articles dealing with the folklore of Western mining camps; to Professor Levette Davidson, director of the Western Folklore Conference, whose studies have covered many aspects of the West; to Miss Caroline Bancroft, who has made a special study of mining-camp lore in Colorado; to Mr. Carl Sandburg, for his contribution mentioned elsewhere in the book; to Mr. John Kelly and his wife, Ethel Kelly, for instruction on the Comstock; to Mr. Eric Kraemer and his wife, Zoray Kraemer, for Six Mile Canyon courtesies; to Professor Grant Loomis, who has made distinct contributions to an understanding of Fred Hart and Dan de Quille; and, finally, to all those real persons whose names are mentioned throughout the body of the book. To them all I am grateful. The credit for any interest which this book may have belongs to such Westerners. For its obvious imperfections I am responsible.

I also wish to express my appreciation to those

who have aided the completion of the book with suggestions, partial reading of the manuscript, typing, and in other ways: Mrs. Rae Korson, Miss Ruth Collins, Commander and Mrs. James G. Clark, Mrs. Jane Amoss, Miss Virginia Holmes, Mr. George Steele, Mr. Cyrus B. Koonce, Mr. Courtney Snyder, and Mr. Herman Norwood.

CONTENTS

xi

PREFACE

As well as anyone else, I am aware that the days of the Wild West have passed, and that civilization —if one cares to call it that—has begun to lay its standardizing hand upon a region which was once free and untrammeled. There still remain, however, out of the past, traditions and customs which distinguish the residents of these states from the residents of others, their way of life from the way of life elsewhere. In spite of the leveling influence of radio, national magazines, and motion pictures, the Westerner lives by a code bred from the land and from his predecessors upon the land. It is a good code and a good way of life. I have attempted to capture something of it in these pages.

This is not a book of history, of social custom, or of folklore. It has something of each, but not enough of any to be considered a "volume" on those subjects. It is reminiscent and introductory. The person who has lived in these states will read it as a book to remind him of a thousand things which are not in this book. The person who has never been there will learn something, I trust, of the past and present pattern of life, and will go on to the reading of the great volumes on the West.

D. E.

IT'S AN OLD
WILD WEST CUSTOM

BETWEEN the Rocky Mountains and the Sierra Nevada, from the Canadian border to Mexico, lies the land which is West. Its chief characteristic is space, the space of great deserts and towering mountains, deep canyons and lonely buttes. It is the space of cloudless days and the vast heavens at night. It is the wild land, torn, gouged, jagged.

Beyond the Sierra to the west lie the rich valleys

and fertile farms of the Pacific Coast, while east of the Rockies the great plains of corn and wheat stretch endlessly across the flat and monotonous land. The land east and west is rich, cultivated, watered. The land between the mountains is dry, barren, wind-swept. To some it is desolate, the end of creation, a God-forsaken waste existing only as a barrier between civilized regions. To those who have settled there, however, it is a mountain and desert paradise, than which there is no other.

All who have looked upon the land—from Escalante, Carson, Jedediah Smith, and the Jayhawkers to the modern tourist—have gazed with awe and wonder. Even those who live there year in and year out cannot look upon it with casual acceptance, cannot ignore it. For the land dominates and shapes them, creating their way of life. And it is never the same land. The mountains and the deserts change with the seasons and shift with the hours of each day. Where there was gold, there is suddenly purple and crimson, and where a mountain was white and shining, it is now black, sullen, and treacherous. The land is changeless and changing, the immutability of a hundred thousand years and the shadow of the moment.

The area of this West is vast even in terms of the continent. The eight states which comprise it—Arizona, New Mexico, Colorado, Utah, Nevada, Idaho, Montana, and Wyoming—include more than three-quarters of a million square miles, 863,887, to be exact. But their combined population is only about half that of New York City—a little more than four million, roughly four and one-half persons per square mile! Texas, which boasts of its size, is crowded in terms of per-capita space when compared with any of these eight states, and shrinks to insignificance in this respect beside Nevada, with its one person per square mile against Texas' twenty.

The traveler who approaches the West of the mountains and Great Basin from virtually any point is aware that he is entering upon a new land. Coming from the east, the level plains slowly give way to eroded hills, the vegetation changes, and tumbleweed and sagebrush replace corn and prairie grass, the land rises imperceptibly mile after mile, and then, vaguely, on the horizon, there are tall clouds—stationary, unlike other clouds. More miles and the clouds resolve themselves into the snow-capped peaks of the Rockies, a gigantic barrier stretching across the continent, passable by early wagon only over the South Pass of the high Wyoming plateau or circuitously out of Trinidad, Colorado, and over Raton Pass to the south and Santa Fe.

The Sierra Nevada forms virtually an identical barrier on the west, cut now by roads that wind from the Sacramento Valley to the high passes at Emigrants' Gap, Donner Summit, and beyond

Hangtown, now decorously named Placerville. The roads mount gently and gradually enough through California foothills—planted with orchards of pear, apple, and plum—until they reach the cool mountain heights, heavy with pine and fir, and then plunge precipitously down eastern slopes to Truckee, Reno, Genoa, and the Carson Valley. The range may be by-passed to the south by way of the Yuma road into Arizona, but where the barrier of the mountains ceases to exist is the heat of the desert in its place, only slightly less than that of Death Valley to the north.

It is as though Nature herself, to protect man, had ringed the vast area with warning barriers: "Only the strong shall enter."

Certain it is that of those who first crossed the land only the strong survived.

The emigrants' highways to the West were the few rivers which penetrated the country, the Green in Wyoming, the Snake in Idaho, the Humboldt in Nevada, the Purgatoire—or Picketwire as the Americans called it—in southern Colorado. And woe be to the traveler and pioneer who left the water routes for nebulous short cuts! The Reed-Donner party in 1846 took the so-called Hasting's Cutoff to the south and west of Salt Lake, roughly the route of the present highway across the salt flats, rather than turning north toward the headwaters of the Humboldt. Already delayed by earlier misfortunes on the trail, the salt desert further impeded their advance for a fatal week, so that when they reached the foothills of the Sierra, winter suffering and death were largely their fate.

Of the original party of ninety persons, only forty-eight survived to reach California. Six died on the route to the Sierra Nevada, and the remaining thirty-six perished from exposure and starvation in the blizzards and deep snows of the mountains. Suffering from snow blindness, footsore, freezing at night, and tortured by hunger during the day, the scene of their pathetic winter camps was one of hopeless agony and horror. To survive, they ate their moccasins, the strings of their snowshoes, and the ox hides which were all that was left of the beasts that had carried them across the plains. In final desperation the party resorted to cannibalism, and the bodies of five who had died and two Indian guides who were killed were eaten.

"The men finally mustered up courage to approach the dead. With averted eyes and trembling hand, pieces of flesh were severed from the inanimate forms and laid upon the coals. It was the very refinement of torture to taste such food, yet those who tasted lived. . . . Human beings were never called upon to undergo more trying ordeals. Dividing into groups, the members of each family were spared the pain of touching their own kindred. Days and perhaps weeks of starvation were awaiting them in the future, and they dare not neglect to provide as best they might. Each of the four bodies was divested of its flesh, and the flesh was dried . . ."

Another party of seven wagons, recklessly and obstinately breaking away from the main train, turned south from Salt Lake in 1849 across the Nevada desert, and, after weary months of traveling, entered the Amargosa Desert area near present-day Beatty, culminating their disastrous journey with the trials of Death Valley. Women and children accompanied the emigrants. William Lewis Manly, who scouted for the Bennett-Arcane wagons, reported their trials:

"The four children were crying for water but there was not a drop to give them. The mothers were nearly crazy, for they expected the children to choke with thirst and die in their arms, and they would rather perish themselves than suffer the agony of seeing their little ones gasp and slowly die. . . .

"This camp of trouble, of forlorn hope, on the edge of a desert stretching out before us like a small sea, with no hope for relief except at the end of a struggle which seemed almost hopeless, is more than any pen can paint, or at all describe. There were no jokes, no mirth, and everyone seemed to feel that he was very near the end of his life, and such a death as stood before them, choking, starving in a desert, was the most dreary outlook I ever saw."

Where men had food, their mouths were so dry that they could not eat. With plenty, some starved to death. Individuals who wandered from their parties were found dead of thirst in the desert. "Wealth was of no value here. A hoard of twenty-dollar gold pieces could now stand before us the whole day long with no temptation to touch a single coin, for its very weight would drag us nearer death."

To the north on the main route across central Nevada, where the Humboldt runs into the sands leaving a desperate stretch of seventy-five miles with no water and nothing but a sandy waste, the emigrants discarded precious belongings which had been carried thousands of miles. Almost within sight of the waters of the Carson and the Truckee, they threw away family belongings—guns, Bibles, saws, mining equipment, bureaus, mirrors, clocks, and anything which might add weight to the wagons—and the desert was strewn with wreckage. Here oxen died and the wagons were left while emigrants pressed forward on foot. Ragtown took its name from the clothes which emigrants discarded once the final passage of the desert had been made.

Alonzo Delano's description of the Black Rock Desert crossing, still farther north, was duplicated in sight and sound along all the trails of western Nevada: "As I walked on slowly and with effort, I encountered a great many animals, perishing for want of food and water, on the desert plain. Some would be gasping for breath, others unable to stand would issue low moans as I came up, in a most distressing manner, showing intense agony. And still others, unable to walk, seemed to brace themselves up on their legs to prevent falling, while here and there a poor ox, or horse, just able to drag himself along, would stagger toward me with a low sound as if begging for water."

The chief impression retained from early accounts of the crossing was the hardship due to lack of water. Where water was important as a route and highway to the early traveler, it is equally important today, and frequently for the same reasons. The prospector moves only where water is apt to be found. Roads and highways link one supply of water to another, a spring to an oasis, the crossing of a river to a distant well. The lack of water has kept great areas unsettled and unexplored. There are vast portions of the land which have not been mapped. And the population, dependent on water, has been held to a minimum. Westerners are aware of this as a determining factor in their way of life, and are more likely than not to bless the dryness of the land, which preserves to them an individual independence not enjoyed elsewhere.

As water is a factor in determining the way of life, so are the mountains. There is virtually no place a traveler can stop without being in sight of mountains on all sides. The desert occupies a good half of the area, but the bulk of the remaining land is made up of mountains, high plateaus, and uplands. To call the Nevada-Utah territory between the Wasatch Mountains and the Sierra Nevada the Great Basin is, in effect, to misname it for the person who has not visited the land. It is true that the whole land, including Arizona and New Mexico, was once a great inland sea, a gigantic basin of water, but under the waters of the sea were high peaks, mountains, and plateaus; the present waters of the Great Salt Lake were a thousand feet higher, and the waters lapped for thousands of years against the Wasatch rim and Pilot Peak in Nevada and the mountains near Wendover. It is as if the waters of the Atlantic were suddenly to dry. The land disclosed might be considered a "basin" in terms of the present continents that flank it, but within itself it would contain mountain ranges, valleys, heights, and depths.

The mountains act as barriers, isolating one section of the land from another, separating the life of the Western Slope from that of the Eastern Slope in Colorado, demarking California from Nevada, dividing Idaho and Montana. They shape the route of the highways, limiting their number to the few passes. But barriers though the mountains may be to travel and communication, they do not hem in or crowd upon the land. They are vast distances in themselves, set between desert and sky, and there is a spaciousness about them which is not found in the hills of New England or the range of the Appalachians. Their barrenness contributes to this effect. Even when heavily timbered, there are the open spaces of lakes, long valleys stretching out to other ranges, the sheer blocks of gray granite, and gaping mountain wounds torn by angry slides of snow and earth.

Characterized by mountain and desert, the land within itself is varied and changing. From the petrified forests of Utah and Arizona to the rich valleys and mountain pastures of Colorado and Idaho, there is always diversity. The great earth upheavals, the ceaseless lapping of the inland seas and lakes, the erosion of wind and storm, and the cruel beating of the sun have all combined to create the varied landscape of the West. Monument Valley, the Royal Gorge, the Painted Desert, Bryce Canyon, the Garden of the Gods, the Grand Canyon, the Great Salt Lake, Cathedral Rocks, and the Yellowstone—these are some of the truly spectacular, if self-consciously named, parts of the land.

But where can the traveler draw the line to say that this is impressive and that is not? The sun going down on an unnamed mountain in Montana, a sudden thundershower over the hills east of Reno, the implacable and shimmering heat making a mirage of an alkali flat, the twisted growth of trees near timber line—where will the observant draw the line?

The Westerner himself need not. He loves the entirety of the land.

IN THE days of the old West, before the advent of the buffalo hunter and the Sharp's rifle, herds of American bison moved across the land. Without strict migratory instincts or patterns, they moved from feeding ground to fresher feeding ground, the tall buffalo grass shoulder high before them, matted and crushed under as the herd moved over it. The herds were enormous, beyond present conception. They moved in small groups of a hundred or a thousand, coalescing slowly, the many into the one, until one vast mass witnessed by early trappers stretched twenty-five miles wide across its front and more than fifty miles in length. Horace Greeley, on his Western trip, saw one herd in which he estimated there were a million buffalo. The sound of their hoofs and the noise of the herd on the move was a vast, rumbling thunder. And it was a good sound to the ear of the Apache and the Sioux, the Cheyenne and the Arapaho and Ute. They hunted the buffalo for winter meat and robes, killing them primitively with arrows and spears, driving them into prepared traps, herding them over cliffs. And the buffalo hunt was a ritual, a great ritual, because the success of the hunt meant the life of the tribe.

But the white hunter came as a matter of business, as he had once come for beaver. In one decade, from 1870 to 1879, the herds were wiped out. Where there had been twenty million buffalo, the hunters themselves, returning to the kill in 1879, were appalled to find that in the whole West there remained only a few thousand. The slaughter had been complete. And it had been a matter of slaughter. Men had killed simply for the hide. Others had killed only for the buffalo tongue. Still others had killed for "sport," riding on special excursion trains into the buffalo country and pumping bullets into the animals as the train moved slowly through the herds. And still others had killed as a matter of Government policy—"If there are no buffalo, the Indians will stay upon the reservations, cease to be nomadic, and depend upon the soil."

Reservations had been set aside for the Indians and, by solemn treaty, these reservations and much marginal land belonged to them as living and hunting grounds. But the buffalo hunter invaded the reservations. And he was followed by the gold hunter. American troops protected both, pushing the Indians back and back, narrowing the domain which had been theirs from time immemorial. There was no peace; there was no treaty that could be believed. "The only good Indians are dead Indians"—to be killed like the buffalo.

On the morning of November 29, 1864, Colonel John Chivington, with 750 soldiers and a howitzer battery, marched through a raging blizzard against a sleeping camp of 650 Arapaho and Cheyenne who had previously surrendered peacefully at Fort Lyon and there been turned away by Major Anthony, who said he could not feed them. This was winter on Sand Creek, and in the lodges were 450 women and children. Colonel Chivington and his volunteer soldiery surrounded the sleeping Indians and, on his specific orders to "spare no one," attacked. Lieutenant Cramer, of the First Colorado Cavalry, reported that "the slaughter was continuous; no Indian, old or young, male or female, was spared."

How many were killed is unknown, but estimates ran as high as five hundred. There were no prisoners taken, and the bodies were horribly mutilated. It was properly termed a massacre—the Sand Creek Massacre—and, however much Chivington's apologists cite his other actions and explain this away, his name is infamous for it in the history of the West. Kit Carson, who had no great love for the Indian, was revolted. So was the country as a whole, but Chivington, although he was cited for court martial, was never even censured.

Again, on March 17, 1876, Colonel Reynolds, with six troops of cavalry, attacked the camp of the Oglala Sioux in the valley of the Powder River. The temperature was forty degrees below zero. The Indians were routed without a moment's preparation and the tepees burned. Women and children froze to death, but the braves rallied and followed the troops, who became panic-stricken. The Indians recovered their ponies and stole the beef cattle of the soldiery. Defeat had, in a measure, been turned into victory.

Pressed as they were on all sides, the Indians struck back in desperation. From the Apache and Comanche in the South to the Cheyenne and Sioux in the North, the last war drums beat along the frontier.

Word went out among the Sioux in the North to gather at the Little Big Horn. Whether, in June,

What Custer did after Reno attacked has been a subject of raging debate ever since. Some say that he circled behind a ridge, distant from the river and out of sight of it, in order to attack the encampment from the far end, and that in doing so he deliberately left Reno and his men to their fate without waiting to observe the result of Reno's attack. Others claim that Custer moved forward to attack on the flank, but that as he progressed with his troops, he remained in sight of the battle across the river and below him.

What he saw, or learned, appalled him. Reno and his three troops forded the stream toward the Sioux lodges, riding at a fast trot across the level flat beyond the Little Big Horn. On one side was the stream, and on the other, low brush. On both sides and in front of Reno were the Sioux, and when he was sufficiently advanced, the Indians attacked. Reno and his troops were cut to ribbons, and had to retreat across the Little Big Horn to a low hill where they entrenched themselves, to fight there a night and a day until reinforcements came. And to lose fifty-six dead and fifty-nine wounded.

Custer, aware now perhaps of the terrible danger in which he stood, sought to secure a position on the most elevated hill in order to defend himself and his men. Custer may have been foolhardy to begin with—Westerners assert that he was—but he died bravely. But the odds were so great that nothing availed him. The Oglalas, the Uncpapas, and the Cheyennes, under Crazy Horse, Gall, and Two Moon, struck with all the savage fury of the fiercest Indian tribes, and the battle was over in less than half an hour. Two hundred and twenty-five soldiers, with Custer, died without having had time to form in anything resembling a defensive battle line. Hoka hey! "It was like chasing buffalo."

The death of Custer and his men, however, was not a massacre. He and his men were soldiers on a mission of war, well-armed, hunting for the enemy, and precipitating the attack. They found what they had come for. And the victorious Sioux, as they packed their lodges and trailed into the Big Horn Mountains from the battleground, composed a song of victory in memory of the battle which has been chanted by the Sioux ever since:

Long Hair, you have found what you were seeking—Death!

The Ute fought and the Paiute, the Arapaho and the Nez Percé, the Papago and the Pima, the Comanche and Apache. Their battles were brief raids, ill-organized, opportunistic. The Indians failed to follow up advantages when they had them, and had no concept of the forces against which they were fighting. To them any intruder not of their own people was an enemy, and they could have no understanding of the fact that in back of a lone wagon train stood a nation on the march.

As the flood of empire moved West in a steady, growing stream, the Indians, pitifully attempting to adjust their own destiny to the assured destiny of the whites they saw passing endlessly before them on the trails, even dreamed of moving to the East, because "there the land must be empty of people."

In the South, the chief warriors were the Chiricahua and Warm Springs Apache. They had counted great names among their leaders—Cochise, Mangas Coloradas—who had terrorized New Mexico and Arizona. And in the '80's, during the last outbreaks, they were led by equally great fighting men—Victorio, Nachez, Chihuahua, Chato, Nana, and the dreaded Geronimo.

Much fiction and many war-whooping motion pictures have so distorted the facts of the Apache raids that Americans now have a confused notion of thousands and thousands of Indians riding on the warpath under Geronimo. Only with truth and the real facts can we gauge the genius of the Apache for war and his incredible feats in the vast spaces of Arizona, New Mexico, and old Mexico.

There were two great outbreaks of the Apache, in 1883 and again in 1885, both led by Geronimo. Most of the Apaches were reconciled to the life of the reservations, and many even served with American troops attempting to capture Geronimo and his followers, who included Chato and Nachez. But Geronimo was restless and would not be contained.

Against Geronimo in the campaign of 1885-1886, lasting eighteen months, were engaged five thousand regular and irregular soldiers, five hundred Indian scouts, and the hostile citizenry of the whole region, not including Mexican forces sent against him in the wild Sierra Madre country. Geronimo's total forces numbered thirty-five men! And they were hampered by the constant necessity of providing for more than one hundred women and children who had left the reservation with them.

Geronimo's total losses, including women and children, were eleven, but not one of these was killed by regular troops. Nor was Geronimo or any of his band ever captured. When he and his followers, harried and harassed, decided that they had had enough, they agreed to parleys—the time and place for which they set themselves—and voluntarily surrendered. Fortunate indeed, for New Mexico and Arizona, that the fifteen hundred Apache men capable of bearing arms did not follow Geronimo from the Fort Apache and San Carlos reservations. The thirty-five were scourge enough. Half of that force, on one occasion only and in a period of six days, traveled four hundred miles in Arizona, killing twenty-six people and driving off stock.

Similarly, in the north, Chief Joseph of the Nez Percé Indians was ordered by the United States Government to leave his lands and to go with his tribe to the Fort Lapwai reservation of Idaho. Hating to do so, yet realizing the uselessness of war, Joseph complied; but on the march to the reservation, younger warriors accused Joseph of cowardice, and without his authority or approval attacked settlers in the valleys of the Salmon and Snake Rivers. The war for which he had not asked had come to his people, who had previously been among the most peace-loving of the tribes. Once begun, however, Chief Joseph assumed full responsibility for the war, and from June, 1877, until October 5, he displayed a rare generalship which outwitted and defeated the cavalry pursuing him. On four separate occasions, across the width and length of Idaho and Montana, he defeated American troops. At the last, with thinning ranks of warriors, he strove desperately to reach the safety of the Canadian border. But in the Bear Paw Mountains of Montana, within sight of Canada, he was cut off by cavalry commanded by General Nelson Miles. Here, in bitter cold and blizzard, his weakened braves fought for more than a week before the inevitable surrender. "It is cold and we have no blankets. The little children are freezing to death. I am tired. My heart is sick and sad. From where the sun now stands, I will fight no more forever." They surrendered, only to be shipped to Kansas, where they succumbed to disease, and from there in freight cars to Oklahoma, where they died. These were mountain Indians. They died on the plains.

In an official account of United States policy toward the Indian in the whole West, General Phil Sheridan had the courage to admit and the distasteful task of reporting that: "The Government made treaties, gave presents, made promises, none of which were honestly fulfilled. We took away their country and their means of support, broke up their mode of living, their habits of life, introduced disease and decay among them, and it was for this and against this they made war."

And the last "war" which they made, the last dream of coups and scalps, grew out of the prophetic Ghost Dance of a Paiute Indian in Nevada and ended under the withering fire of Hotchkiss guns at Wounded Knee. Wovoka, an Indian on the Walker Lake reservation, dreamed a dream in which the Creator gave him a dance to teach to other Indians. The dance was one which would bring power to the red man, death to the whites, and the return of the buffalo. "The buffalo are coming. They cover the earth. . . ." Buckskin shirts with embroidered buffalo and eagle designs would render the bullets of the soldiers harmless.

First performed in Nevada in January, 1889, the Ghost Dance swept the West. The Utes learned of it, and the Blackfeet, the Shoshone, the Cheyennes, and the Sioux. Tribal emissaries were sent from Montana and Idaho and from as far away as the

Dakotas to learn the dance and to teach it to the tribes. Thousands of Indians learned it and began deserting the reservations to gather in the Bad Lands with the Sioux chiefs, Kicking Bear and Short Bull. Big Foot and Yellow Bird, with three hundred and fifty followers, attempted to join them, but the by-now-alerted Seventh Cavalry intercepted them and ordered the Sioux band to make camp on Wounded Knee Creek. The Indians seemed peaceful and at Wounded Knee were at first allowed to keep their arms. But military caution finally prevailed, and on the morning of December 29, 1890, the soldiers, under the protection of Hotchkiss guns, began disarming the one hundred and twenty warriors of the Sioux.

During the slow process of collecting the arms, Yellow Bird began the Ghost Dance. "Bullets cannot pierce your shirts. . . ." Suddenly he threw a handful of dust in the air and donned his war bonnet. Killing began at once. The Hotchkiss guns created frightful havoc, hurling explosive shells into the massed camp. In the brief carnage, sixty soldiers and two hundred Indian men, women, and children died.

The Ghost Dance craze ended on the frontier. And so did all dream of buffalo. And the sound of drums.

THE WESTERNER left his names casually
and naturally upon the land. Only rarely in these
states are the self-conscious names found—the
Thermopolis of Montana, the Tempe and Phoenix
of Arizona, the amusing and pretentious Copper-
opolis. By and large they are names from the land,
the plants and animals, the watering holes and
creeks, the mountains and natural formations. They
are also the names drawn from experiences, un-

usual or disastrous, and words borrowed from the
Indians or retained from the Spanish and French.

The record of the names identifies the land. This
was cattle and mining country, a land of little water
and of mountains, a land of hardship and humor.
From the sonorous La Villa Real de la Santa Fe de
San Francisco to the clipped Jerked Beef Butte, the
names are West.

A rancher in Greenlee County, Arizona, killed
seventy rattlesnakes in a sloping valley under the
Mogollon Rim and gave it the name Rattlesnake
Basin. Wild Horse Canyon was a place for the
roundup of horses, and Horse Thief Basin a hide-
out for rustlers. Cowboys saw a white horse—actually a mare—ranging a particular group of hills;
the mare gave birth to several colts similarly colored, and the place took its name, White Horse
Hills. A settler's sheep were attacked and slaughtered by a wildcat, and Wildcat Canyon was the
result. Gobbler Point was a favorite rendezvous for
wild turkeys, and Buzzard Roost Mesa for buzzards.
The Big Horn Mountains and the Big Horn River
of Wyoming and Montana are named for the Rocky
Mountain bighorn sheep. Antelope Peak and the
valley and creek bearing the same name in Yavapai
County, Arizona, were christened by an early traveler: "I killed three antelope and we gave the
peak this name." Coyote Creek, Grizzly Peak, and
Eagle Nest Mountain are clear, and Vinegaron Well

borrows the Spanish word for the whip-tail scor-
pion. The Cimarron Mountains, famous in many
"westerns," comes from the Spanish word meaning
wild or outlaw, but Mexicans call the mountain
sheep *cimarron*, so the reader has his choice.

Badger and Soap Creeks, which rise under the
Vermilion Cliffs in Coconino County, Arizona, are
close together and were named by Jacob Hamblin,
an early Mormon pioneer. Hamblin killed a badger
on one creek and proceeded to the second where he
cleaned the animal and put it to boil. Instead of the
stew which he expected to find in the morning,
however, the alkali in the water and the fat from
the badger resulted in a kettle of soap, so he named
the two creeks Badger and Soap. And Methodist
Creek was not named by any pious preacher trek-
king westward to save souls. A cowboy in 1890
wandered up the creek to find a bee tree which he
proceeded to rob but very shortly had to abandon
in high-tail flight. "The way the bees went after
me would have made a Methodist preacher swear!"
The town of Bumble Bee in Arizona was similarly
named, and Big Bug Creek was identified in 1863
by prospectors who found large water bugs, or
skippers, sailing over its surface. Bear Wallow
Creek, which rises in the Blue Range and flows into
Black River, was named for the numerous bears
that came to the cool wallows to fight the flies tor-
menting them.

In the Southwest there are towns named Cactus, Cholla, Ocotillo, and Cedar for the varieties of cactus and for the scrub cedar that distinguish the landscape. Cottonwood Springs and Cottonwood Wash were landmarks for the early pioneers searching for water. Aspen, Colorado, once a mining camp and now a resort, takes its name from the trees with the trembling leaves. Alder Gulch, scene of the gold strike which brought a boom to southwestern Montana, was named simply for the alders which flanked the gulch. White Sage Wash and Greasewood Mountain could only be in the West.

Other watering holes and tanks, creeks and rivers, took their names from the nature of the land or from experiences of pioneers. Desert Wells, Clay Springs, Steamboat Springs, Sand Creek, Salt Well, Salt Marsh, Rock Springs, Little Cottonwood Creek, and Gravelly Ford are descriptive enough of the nature of the places. Missoula is the Salish Indian for "by the chilling waters," and Powder River takes its name from the fine, gunpowder-black sand characterizing it. Disappointment Creek and Humbug Creek were branded for posterity by unlucky prospectors. And the beautiful name of Silver Plume, near Idaho Springs in Colorado, comes not from the mountain streams flowing nearby, but from the feathery nature of the silver ore found in the mines. Freezeout Creek in hot Arizona country also has nothing to do with the weather, but comes from the game of freezeout poker which cowboys habitually played there. Ambush Water Pocket was the result of an Indian attack in which three white men were killed in Mohave County, Arizona, in 1869; and a dead emigrant was found at Deadman Tank. The name Arizona itself comes from the Papago Indian term *aleh-zon,* meaning a small spring, and the particular springs in question are near Banera, eight miles south of the border and eighty-five below Tucson.

Distances and the formation of the land were important as landmarks to early settlers and pioneers, who had no maps to go by. Consequently, there is a plethora of names suggested by curious rock formations or the accurate measurements of previous travelers. There is Six Mile Canyon near Virginia City, Nevada; Seven Mile Creek in Gila County, Arizona; Hundred and Fifty Mile Canyon, and Four Mile Peak—not four miles high, but four miles distant from Biscuit Peak. Mitten Peak looks like a mitten. Descriptive also are Sawed Off Mountain, Sombrero Butte, Elephant Head and Elephant Butte, Battleship Mountain, Ox Yoke Mountain, Rabbit's Ear Pass, Camelback Mountain, Cinch Hook Butte, and Pyramid Lake, with its perfect rock pyramid rising above the water. There were numerous Black Mesas, Red Buttes, Dry Washes— both Big and Little—and an occasional interesting variant, such as Midnight Mesa.

There are names marking westward expansion, the names of trappers, explorers, Indians with whom the whites came in friendly or warlike contact, and the historic names of forts and wars. Kit Carson, who traveled the whole West, gave his name to the Carson River and Carson City in Nevada and to a National Forest in New Mexico. There are the Fremont and Sevier Rivers in Utah, Walker Lake in Nevada, and Pikes Peak in Colorado. Denver, Reno, Cody, Custer, Desmet, and Meeker are cities and towns named for men who helped shape the West's history, some with ignorance and stupidity, some with vision. Ouray, Colorado, and Winnemucca, Nevada, commemorate friendly chiefs of different Ute tribes, and Utah takes its name from the Indian nation. The Shoshone, Blackfoot, Apache and Cheyenne Indians are remembered with towns in Idaho, Arizona, and Wyoming. The forts of expansion dot the maps: Fort Morgan and Fort Collins in Colorado, Fort Churchill in Nevada, Laramie and Bridger in Wyoming, Fort Sumner and old Fort Union in New Mexico.

The extent of Mormon influence and the domain of their inland empire is marked on the maps with names drawn from the Book of Mormon: Moroni, Lehi, Manti, Nephi, and Alma—the angels, prophets, and kings. The Jordan River flows south of Salt Lake, and the town of Moab is near the Colo-

rado line. And because the Mormons, a friendly
and tightly-knit people, were accustomed to calling
each other by given names rather than family
names—"Brother Ephraim" or "Brother George"
—they named their towns by first names as well:
Brigham, Heber, Ephraim, and Hyrum.

The curious traveler can also chart with reasonable accuracy the extent of Spanish penetration
from Mexico to the north and the westward movement of French trappers simply by checking the
names on the land. From Las Cruces, New Mexico,
the tide of Spanish conquest and exploration moved
north into central Colorado, where the Spanish
names begin to peter out at La Junta and Pueblo
and where the line ends at Buena Vista, Salida, and
the northern reaches of the Sangre de Cristo Mountains. The names are rich in legend and history:
Socorro, Belén, Albuquerque, Santa Fe, Alamogor-
do, Santa Rosa, Trinidad. There is strength to the
roll of the Spanish words, proud as the small companies of men who traveled north over the plains
and who first saw the snowy ranges and the long
valleys.

In Arizona, the Spanish names move north by
way of the San Pedro and Gila Rivers, north from
Nogales, Casa Grande, Mesa, and by way of San
Francisco Peak into southern Utah. Here the line
ends abruptly save for the memory of Escalante's
expedition in 1776—a town is named for him—and

for the American name of Spanish Forks, south of
Salt Lake, which the Spaniards never saw. The
land was barren and dry, poorer than the land to
the south. And so was Nevada, and the Spanish
names there are few—Las Vegas, Alamo, Caliente,
the Amargosa Desert—the bitter desert—all in the
south. But the great rivers that rise in the Rockies
and flow through the dry states to the sea, one to
the Pacific and one to the Atlantic, were named by
them—the Rio Grande and the Colorado. So also
were the mountains to the west, from which Nevada takes its name.

They named small places and landmarks, just as
the later Americans were to do. Polvo, four miles
east of Tucson, is in dry, dusty country, while Pozo
Verde and Pozo Muchos marked a green well
and many wells. Tierra Amarilla was the yellow
ground, Sierra Blanca the white range. And the
Camino del Diablo was the Devil's Highway, rightly named, for over its stretch from Sonora to the
Gila River near Yuma more than three thousand
travelers from the south perished for lack of water.

In Idaho, to the north, there are the French
names: Portneuf, Malheur, Coeur d'Alene, Pend
d'Oreille, Nez Percé, Gros Ventre, names given to
rivers, lakes, and Indian tribes. And Boise is not
Boise, but *Les Bois!*, shouted happily by an early
trapper whose accent was something less than that

of Paris, but whose pleasure at seeing the "woods" was unmixed.

Americans who came West were patriotic and proud of their heritage, Yankee or Confederate. Uncle Sam Hill, Old Glory, American Flag, and American Flats took their places on the map. Virginia City, Montana, was almost Varina—for the wife of Jefferson Davis—until a Northerner said, "I'll see you damned first!" Virginia City, Nevada, was named by James Fennimore or Finney, one of its early prospectors. Filled to the ears with local whisky, he fell down and broke a bottle. As a Virginian, he rose with Southern dignity and spirit to make good use of the spilled liquid: "I christen this town Virginia!" Men from Virginia City carried its name to a mining camp in Arizona and to Virginia Canyon between Central City and Idaho Springs in Colorado. All camps wanted to enjoy the luck of the Comstock Lode, and Virginia City, Montana, received its final name from the reputation of Nevada's.

The names of the mining camps begin with the rather standard and hopeful "Gold" and "Silver" and are found in all the states: Gold Hill, Gold Flat, Goldfield, Gold Run, Gold Point, and Gold Springs; Silver City, Silver Creek, Silver Glance, Silver Hill, and Silverton. There are names also appropriate to mining aspirations: Oro and Oro Blanco, Eureka, Golconda, Ophir, and Bonanza. Nostalgic miners

named places for the states and cities from which
they had come—Delaware Flats, California Gulch,
Springfield City, Missouri City, and Nevadaville,
all in Colorado.

But there were other towns and mining districts,
equally rich in tradition, bearing names known
throughout the West: Tombstone, Creede, Tonopah, Central City, Butte, Leadville, Ely, Bisbee, and
Jerome. Ed Schieffelin, who discovered Tombstone,
was warned by friends not to prospect in the southern Arizona region because of the dreaded Apache.
"They'll lift your scalp and all you'll find will be
your tombstone." So Tombstone the camp became,
when Schieffelin struck it rich. A prospector in
another area, finding a round ball of silver nine
inches in diameter and worth $12,000, named the
site of his lucky strike Globe.

Cripple Creek was named because of the cattle
which crippled themselves in the bog holes, and
Fairplay was hopefully christened by miners who
insisted on fair play in the diggings. Telluride took
its name from the tellurous ores, and Bannack from
an Indian tribe. Tarryall was named by miners who
struck it rich in an unexpected spot, all deciding
to tarry and explore the ground further. And Tin
Cup was christened by the prospector who panned
the first gold from a drinking cup, the town name
setting a modest standard for the later adjoining
settlements of Iron Cup, Silver Cup, and Gold Cup.

THE MEN who discovered the mines showered names upon them with the same largesse with which they tossed "dust" over the bar, whimsically and be damned to you, hopefully and for the hell of it. They staked their claims with humor, imagination, sentiment, patriotism, and wishful thinking. The miner had no one to consult but himself, and his "so be it" was law to the map makers who came after him.

37

Take Ed Schieffelin, with his discovery of Tombstone. His brother, Al, said to him, "You're a lucky
cuss." So Schieffelin named his mine the Lucky
Cuss. When N. C. Creede located his first rich mine
in Colorado, his partners shouted happy profani-
ties. But Creede himself was not a cussing character. The best he could do, seeing the ore, was to
exclaim, "Holy Moses!" And Holy Moses the mine
became.

Again, in Montana, two partners had agreed not
to name their claim until they struck pay dirt. One
of them, weary, left his work to nap during an
afternoon, but the other continued puttering
around in the prospect hole. Digging away, he
came on a body of glistening ore. Scrambling out
of the hole and up the hillside, he shouted excitedly
to his partner, "Wake up, Jim, we've struck it!"
And the mine took its name, Wake Up Jim.

Just as the camps themselves had been opti-
mistically named—Ophir, Bonanza—so the mines
were frequently christened for luck. After all, who
was to say that the prospector might not become
a Plutocrat or Gold King, and his wife a silver or
Copper Queen? They boasted of their fabulous fu-
tures, naming them Bullion and Champion, Mammoth and Ton a Minute. There was the Long Lode
and the undisputed Matchless, the High Ore and
the Hidden Treasure, the Little Giant and the Tip
Top. In New Mexico, the Millionaire Mine set a

not unreasonable limit to the finder's aspirations.
And in Nevada there is the cocky Jumbo Gold—in
the Awakening Mining District of the Slumbering
Hills.

But other miners were cautious and skeptical.
They had found "country rock" too often and, like
the Greeks, had no desire to tempt fate with brags
and boasts. They named their mines the Humbug,
the Midget, and the Speculator, the Poorman, Last
Dollar, and Last Chance. And one miner on Canyon Creek, in the Coeur d'Alene district of Idaho,
bluntly named his claim the Ore-Or-No-Go, a put
up or shut up exhortation to himself and Mother
Earth.

Of the men who named their mines patriotically,
Winfield Scott Stratton deserves the crown. Stratton had followed Cowboy Bob Womack's discovery
of gold into Cripple Creek in 1891 and located rich
mines throughout the district. Beginning with the
Independence, he named them the Washington,
Abe Lincoln, Madison, White House, American Eagle, Yankee Girl, and Plymouth Rock. A lone South-
erner raised the Blue Flag there in isolated protest,
and received strong support to the north, where the
famous Robert E. Lee helped to make Leadville a
boom camp. At Telluride there was the Liberty
Bell, and in Utah the Yankee, and Uncle Sam at
Eureka. The Coeur d'Alene had its Bunker Hill,
and White Oaks, New Mexico, its Old Abe.

By and large, however, the miners were more sentimental about their wives, sweethearts, and local loves than about the American past. Without exception, every camp can claim mines honoring the ladies. In Butte alone there are the Emma, Nettie, Cora, Alice, Minnie Jane, Minnie Healy, and Little Minah. Cripple Creek, too, outweighed its patriotism with the Ada Bell, Theresa, Mary Nevin, Mollie Kathleen, Little Ida, Orpha May, Mary McKinney, and Rose Nicol. Anna J. was serious enough as a name, but Fanny B. Mine was christened with evident humor. And was the May B a woman, or a question mark, or both?

Miners also remembered their home town and states. Thomas Cruse's Drumlummon Mine near Marysville, Montana, was named for his native town in Ireland. Jimmy Doyle named the Portland, in Colorado, for his birthplace, Portland, Maine. There are the Shannon, Liverpool, Penobscot, Alabama, Atlanta, Pennsylvania, and Georgia. Miners from earlier diggings and Western towns carried their names to later claims with the Frisco and Sacramento in Idaho, the Deadwood in Cripple Creek, and the Crown Point in Arizona from Gold Hill's mine in Nevada.

As the towns had been named for animals found on the land, so, too, were the mines. A nest of hornets was sufficient cause to christen the famous Yellow Jacket on the Comstock Lode. In Idaho and

Montana there were the Badger, Moose, Wild Horse, and Buffalo. Colorado had its Chicken Hawk and Bluebird mines. But the great Tiger Mine in the Coeur d'Alene took its name not from any Bengal beast but from the traditional nickname for the gambling game of faro.

The time and place of the strike on a claim had much to do with the naming of certain mines. The Moonlight was discovered under the light of a brilliant full moon. There is the Snowstorm Mine near Troy, Montana, and the high Snow Line in Idaho. There are also the Morning and Evening mines in the Coeur d'Alene, and the May Day in Utah.

Mines were, of course, solidly named for their owners or discoverers—the Hale and Norcross, Gould and Curry, the S. Burns and the Gleason— but the more entertaining were those named with individual imagination or out of curious reasoning. The Neversweat in Butte was named by the miners themselves because the workings were kept cool by an unusual current of air. The Anaconda was so called by Michael Hickey, who had read Horace Greeley's account of "Grant's army encircling Lee's forces like a giant anaconda." Two tenderfoot druggists named the rich Pharmacist. In Montana and in Idaho there are the Orphan Boy and the Orphan Girl, claims sadly remote and far distant from all others in their neighborhood. The Mexican on the Comstock was originally a sixth interest of the

Ophir purchased by a Mexican. And the Joe Bowers and the Butcher Boy in Utah recall popular songs which have passed into the folk tradition.

For the majority of the names there are explanations, but there are many whose origins have been lost as the camps were deserted, and their knowledgeable residents drifted on or died. How account, for example, for the Butterfly Terrible, the Bopeep, Wobbly Legs, and Old Lout? The Asteroid stood out like a star from all other claims, and the St. Lawrence was named for the patron saint of two Irishmen. But what of the Gin Shot, the Sun and Moon, the City of Paris, and the You Like?

...AND EACH OTHER

ASMEN named the land and the mines, so they named each other. There was no Mr. William Bonney or Mr. William Cody. There was Billy the Kid and Buffalo Bill, Calamity Jane and Soapy Smith. The land of the West was a democratic leveler. The Mister was dropped and there were no Sirs, and all the name a man needed was an easy and identifying "handle."

They called each other by the familiar first

names—Joe and Charlie, Jim, Mike, Dan, and
Johnny. But as the camps and towns grew, there
were many Joes and Mikes and they needed further identification. The simplest and most natural
way, the very process by which names first came
into being, was to call each other by occupation.
There was Louis the barber, Daley the hatter, Axel
the carpenter, Woodchopper Joe, Jim the smith,
Dutch Louis the butcher, and Bill the bartender.
Bedbug Smith was not lousy—like Lousy Dick or
Never-Wash—but was the much needed extermi-
nator man for the boarding houses at Gold Hill. Old
App the Dutchman, in Butte, sold apples and
grapes, garbling his wares once into the classic and
loudly shouted "Grapples and apes!" And Snowshoe Thompson carried the mail over the Sierra to
Carson, where he was frequently the only winter
contact between residents of the Valley and the
outside world.

The prowess of men at their work earned them
nicknames. Miners were called Jackhammer,
Doublejack, and Singlejack for their proficiency
with mining tools. Ingersoll Slim could outdrill
any man in the Western states, and took his name
from the Ingersoll-Rand drilling machine. He was
the pride of any camp in which he worked, and
lived up to his reputation by wearing $15 silk shirts
while on shift behind the machine. Hardrock Hank
worked the hardrock mines of the West, and Con

the Horse and Mike the Mule were so strong that they thought nothing of pushing loaded ore cars in the Butte mines when their animals were sick.

Apart from their occupations, men were christened for the places and states from which they had come. A cowboy arrived in camp with no name but Pete. Pete? Just Pete. What camp you from? No camp, just Arizona. O.K., Arizona Pete. There was Telluride Joe and Eldorado Johnny, Frisco Kate and Dublin Dan. Powder River Jack hailed from the Powder River country of Montana, and Dixie Munn Skelly—the "Gold Woman" of Central City—came from Louisiana. The mines about which they bragged also gave them names—Cresson Mike, Gold Coin Red, Bullfrog Murphy, and Julia Bob.

Countries of origin entered the nicknames— China Charlie, English George, Nick the Greek, Dutch Louis, Spanish Joe, Frenchy, and plain Swede. One miner with an unpronounceable name was simply referred to as "the new man." He picked it up and explained himself to others, "I'm new man." And Newman he finally became in fact, his Scandinavian name forever lost.

Physical characteristics distinguished them. There was Crooked-Nose Pete and Baldy Golden, Blind Dick, Sleepy Otto, and Dirty-Face Jack. Strawberry Yank sported an alcoholic nose, and Montana's Fat Jack was as lean as a lathe. Three-

Fingered Smith, an early settler on the South Fork of the Salmon River in Idaho, seized an axe and chopped off two fingers that had been bitten by a rattlesnake. Peg-Leg Annie's feet were frozen in a snowstorm on Bald Mountain; she was filled with whisky, tied down, and the feet amputated above the ankles by Tug Wilson, who used a common meat saw and jackknife. Johnny the Giant was big, Stuttering Alex had his troubles, and Diamond-Tooth Baker sported his wealth in a front tooth. Kettle-Belly Brown was prominent on Virginia City's C Street, and Shorty Russell still tends bar.

They were named for unusual actions, events, or peculiarities.

Jimmy July wore an American flag in his lapel and was the only naturalized Chinaman in Butte. Fourth-of-July Murphy raised patriotic Nevada hell on the national holiday. Slot-Machine Ida had a passion for the one-armed bandits, and played the nickel machine whenever she had money. Joe Viani gave her ten dollars one night simply to watch her whoop, howl, and yell at the plums, lemons, and bells. Nickel Annie never bummed anyone for more than a nickel, and Shoestring Annie proclaimed her wares simply and directly— "Buy a pair of shoelaces, you God-damned cheapskate!" Christmas-Tree Murphy killed a man with a Christmas tree. And Bear-Tracks Murphy got his name on the Moffat Tunnel job one winter when he made more than passing love to a foreman's wife. The husband returned unexpectedly, and Murphy leaped out a window and across the snow, while the husband demanded to know of his wife who had been there. "Why, nobody." "Well, what are them tracks there then?" "Them? Them's bear tracks."

Hundred-Dollar Jim never wagered more than once a day, but always bet an even hundred dollars in "dust," which he played straight up on one number in roulette, stopping—win or lose—with that play. Four-Day Jack worked four days in the mines and quit, a record better than that of the usual boomer or "ten-day miner." Dead-Shot Reed, Six-Shooter Brown, and Chickie-Thief the Chinaman are obvious. Crack-'Em- Down Mike was the soul of peace, but uproariously floored a friend once to earn his title. Wheelbarrow Harbert at first protested vigorously when he was propelled home drunk in a barrow at Tin Cup, but soon grew accustomed to it and finally expected the taxi service. And Telephone Tschaikovsky's real name was Matt Konarsky. He earned the Tschaikovsky by plinking out two-fingered tunes on a bar piano, and acquired the Telephone when a fellow miner, happily Irish, saw him in the shower wearing new fangled truss equipment to support a rupture: "Lord God, will ye have a look at the tiliphones on old Tschaikovsky!"

H.A.W. Tabor was known by his initials as "Haw" Tabor, and O.K. Hargraves was naturally "O.K." The Unsinkable Mrs. Brown in Colorado survived the Titanic disaster. Dinger Williams was proficient at "dinging" pool balls into the pockets, and his brother, Doughbelly Williams, as a youngster, asked his father for a chew of tobacco. "Get away from me, you little doughbelly!" Deacon Blake, an old newspaperman, swears an unprintable streak from the right side of an almost toothless mouth. Skiyoomper brags about his "ski yoomping" exploits in the old country. And Bronco Lazzeri, who wouldn't know which side of a horse to climb, is the unbroken and irrepressible bartender-owner of the Union Brewery Saloon on the Comstock.

A natural outcome of the continued use of nicknames was to drive the men's real names into oblivion. Many a cemetery in the West is filled with otherwise nameless Joes, Mikes, and Jims. When death struck suddenly, there was very often the real problem of any name for the victim. A stranger, who provoked a fight in a San Simon, Arizona, saloon in the '80's and fell riddled with bullets, was casually buried under a headstone that was partially informative: "He was a dam fule." Lander and Eureka County court records, in Nevada, contain brief entries—"Bull Dog Kate was stabbed and killed by Hog-Eyed Mary"; "Levi

Maize, *alias* Buffalo Bill, was shot and instantly killed by Flying Dutchman"; "A man known as Fred . . ."

And in the town of Austin, a stage driver carried a letter for a week, hunting for Mr. Charles Brown to whom it was addressed. An old friend finally remembered that Charles Brown was the driver himself, locally known as Stub. Stub protested, "Why in the hell can't they write a man by the name he goes by?"

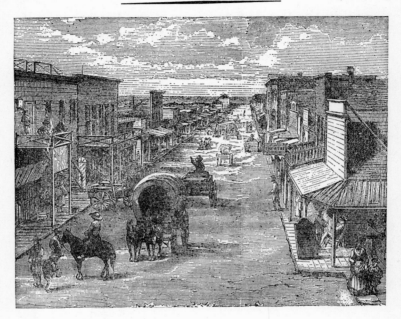

No ONE needed a clairvoyant to know that where gold or silver was discovered, there towns would mushroom into being. And without benefit of trained economists, even the die-hard miner knew that when ore pinched out into borrasca, the reason for a town's existence died also. Ghost towns are scattered over the whole Western landscape. Some of them are utterly and forever desolate and dead; others bravely remember the past

and, like an old man dancing a jig of his youth in
a saloon, deny the death which faces them. The
discovery of gold, the first, hasty construction of
shacks and cabins, the mushroom growth of a boom
town, the later, opulent development into a "city,"
and then the slow, wavering decline into deserted
ruins as the gold was exhausted—this cycle of the
Western mining camp was repeated again and
again, and is still in process. It is a custom determined not by men on the land, but by the limiting
gifts of the land itself.

As the land determined the length of stay, so the
land also determined the locations of the towns.
Where gold or silver was found, there towns grew.
Where oases existed or water crossed the path of
the westward routes to California, towns came into
being. Natural halting places in Indian territory
became forts. The needs of vast cattle ranches
brought settlements into existence.

The cities are few and their origins similar to
those of the towns. Denver began as a supply point
for the Clear Creek mining camps, extending its
commercial tentacles slowly to include the whole
Rockies. There are old-timers today who can remember when antelope grazed on the capitol
grounds, and when the space occupied by the city
itself was a rolling plain without a single man-
planted tree. Salt Lake City was a natural point for
all westward travelers to stop, rest, and re-outfit

before beginning the hazardous desert crossing. Tucson, Phoenix, Albuquerque, and Santa Fe stand on the line of east-west and south-north travel. Helena grew out of the Last Chance Gulch gold strike to become Montana's capital. And Reno supplied the mines to the south and east, Tonopah, Austin, Goldfield, and Rawhide. Few as the cities are, their standardizing influence has been slight, principally, perhaps, because they are in reality still only overgrown towns and are regarded as such even by their discerning residents. There is nothing wrong with this. On the contrary, it is to the credit of each city that society has not had an opportunity yet to shake down, harden, and stratify. To the extent that it does in these Western cities, by so much will the city cut itself off from the heritage of its own past and a common bond of understanding with the people of the small mining camps, cattle towns, and ranches who, in the last analysis, brought the cities into existence and now support them.

The social life of the old West, then, was in its towns. And the physical character of these towns was in large part determined by the location which the land decreed. In general, there are two types: those in the mountains and those on the plains. The mountain towns were the offspring of the gold and silver stampedes. The plains towns were supply points on the line of travel.

The towns in the mountains bunched themselves as best they could into deep canyons, ravines, and gulches. Sometimes a mountain valley, as at Telluride, was wide enough and flat enough to accommodate the town reasonably, but more often the houses staggered precariously up steep hillsides, one street level with the rooftops of houses on the street below. There is a pathetic moan—to the tune of "Auld Lang Syne"—in a stanza from Central City describing the hazards of living on the lower street when youngsters above were given to putting out fires with direct and, sometimes, primitive action:

> Why don't that man bring me some bricks
> To build my chimney higher,
> To keep the boys and girls at night
> From putting out my fire?

These mountain towns were not on any normal route of travel except in rare instances. Roads did not go through them, but had to be built *to* them. Each one was the end of a trail. The existence of each was justified not by its relation to another town on the highway ahead, but by itself alone. In some instances a road would seem to go through these towns, but if the traveler surveys the scene accurately, he will note that in reality the road which seems to continue out of the town is actually a second road *into* the town, meeting the first in the main street. Virginia City, Nevada, and Central City, Colorado, are good examples of this.

The flat towns on the deserts and plains, on the other hand, owe their existence to the main street which, on similar analysis, is not a street at all, but integrally part and parcel of the highway leading on through town. The towns, like "boosters" on the transcontinental telephone system, exist to insure the continuity of the highway and the further journey of the traveler. The main street of Trinidad, Colorado, was and still is part of the historic Santa Fe Trail; and the complete reason for Wendover's existence, on the Nevada-Utah line, is to rest and refresh the traveler journeying east or west after his hard desert drive.

The main street of the plains towns is built like a straightaway racetrack, an admission by the town itself that the visitor's business is temporary and his chief concern that of going on through. The desert or plain is at either end. The Pony Express raced through these towns—a clatter of hoofs, a cloud of dust, a pouch dropped. Stagecoaches stopped briefly. But the road went on through, symbol of the restless and growing West. Only in a handful of towns in the Spanish Southwest is there anything resembling the village square which one finds in the permanent communities of the South and in New England and Pennsylvania. The West was dynamic, not static and settled.

Whether it was as straight as the highway, or

crooked and winding as a gulch or ravine might
dictate, the mountain and plains towns had the
main street in common. When the first phase of
scattered shacks, shanties, tents, lean-tos, wickiups,
and dugouts had passed, when the camp ceased to
be a camp and became a town, the special character of this street became evident. It reflected the
life of the West. First, last, and always, there was
the saloon, not one, but as many as the town could
support. There was no euphemism about it, no law
requiring that the whisky mill hide behind such
terms as "cocktail lounge," "tavern," or "restaurant"—with an ABC license diminutively lettered
on the window. The words were Saloon, Bar, and
Whisky, and they were painted in mammoth letters
on the false fronts, fronts which seem pretentious to
us now, but which served as the advertising billboards of their day. Outside the saloons a wooden
sidewalk, often raised a foot or so from the ground,
separated the buildings from the unpaved, dusty
street. And on the wooden sidewalks, backed
against the buildings, were long benches or a row
of weather-beaten chairs, where customers and
idlers sat to watch the flow of life in the street.

Distinctive of the West, also, were the other
buildings—the Wells, Fargo station, the assay offices of the mining camps, the saddle and leather
goods store of the cow towns, the three-story hotels
and boardinghouses, the volunteer fire department,

the gambling and gaming clubs, the blacksmith shop and corral, the local newspaper office, and the general stores outfitting miners, prospectors, and cattlemen. The buildings were joined together in an unbroken line, the shortage of bricks and lumber requiring that each man take advantage of an already constructed wall against which to build his own establishment. There was no monotony to the street, however, for the false fronts were uneven and ragged, some taller than others, some wider than their neighbors. The bright colors of the buildings—red, orange, green, a desert gray—and the flamboyant, often crude, lettering of the signs gave them added character.

Sometimes on the main street, but more often on an adjoining one, were the courthouse and jail. Churches also were set apart on lots of their own, and the hospital or "pest house" was some distance removed. The red-light district was usually segregated, but not at any great distance from the main street, the saloons, and gambling houses.

The homes of residents varied according to their wealth. Two- and three-story dwellings of brick, or wooden homes with ornate gingerbread scrollwork, were signs of mining-camp affluence. Their interiors were filled with fabulous, heavy furniture, diamond-dust mirrors, marble fireplaces, crystal chandeliers, thick carpets, lace curtains, and expensive bric-a-brac—all imported to distant gulches across the plains from the East or by ship around the Horn. These were the homes of the mine owners and superintendents. The miners and other residents lived more modestly, those who were single living in boardinghouses or hotels, those with families occupying small, one-story houses.

It becomes increasingly difficult, as time destroys the towns, to visualize the scene. The greatness of many of them has been swept away by disastrous fires. Others have collapsed under the weight of winter snows and storms. Still others have been wantonly and shortsightedly looted, merely for old bricks or usable lumber and beams. And still others, surviving in part, have been "modernized" by the residents or businessmen, who have constructed Coney Island-like tourist "attractions" which repel, rather than attract, anyone desiring to know the old West. A person must travel today and take the surviving parts of many towns to reconstruct one whole—a sagging opera house here, a theater there, a fire house with its polished engine and gleaming fire trumpets, a newspaper office with its old press and hand-set type, saloons with their great mahogany bars and gambling equipment, and homes with their once fashionable furnishings. It is still not too late, however, in spite of destruction and dispersion, for a Hearst or a Guggenheim or the citizens of a state to restore to its former physical greatness one of the mining camps, so that it becomes a lasting, historic monument to that phase of Western life.

Through these towns passed the life of the West —prospectors, miners, cattlemen, cowboys, the gay ladies, preachers, cardsharps, gunmen. Looking at a gulch or hillside town, with its few sagging buildings, though, how will the visitor become aware that here life was bright and pulsating? Nature has had its way, and the visitor looks upon the deserted gulch almost as did the first discoverers of gold. How will the tourist know of Oscar Wilde and Adelina Patti, General Grant and Mark Twain, Sarah Bernhardt and Edwin Booth visiting, lecturing, or performing, not in New York, San Francisco, or Washington, but in a ravine in Montana, a desert town on the Mexican border, a gulch in Colorado, a "city" in Nevada? And of the miners who showered small fortunes in silver and gold upon the opera stage for their favorites? Can he conceive now of a single silver lode so great that its production upset the financial world? Or of a vug, a roomlike pocket of gold ore, so rich in a Colorado mine that steel bank-vault doors were built across the tunnel, and the mine, almost in fact, became a bank? Or of Stratton, whose coffers were the workings of the Independence Mine, walking into the Brown Palace Hotel and buying it, lock, stock, and barrel, simply to fire an impertinent

manager who had previously refused him a room
because he was not "properly dressed?" Or of Haw
Tabor, a small grocer become a multi-multi-mil-
lionaire whose financial holdings stretched over
the world, a peddler of flour and shovels, sky-
rocketed into a United States Senator?

The mines boomed. And their boom was the
Aladdin's lamp of the West, and the eyes of the
whole world were turned beyond the Rockies, and
the names of Cripple Creek, Central City, Leadville, Creede, Tombstone, the Coeur d'Alene, Austin, Virginia City, White Pine were on the lips of
men everywhere. Germany, France, and England
sent their best engineers and financial experts to
see and to estimate and to report. They came and
they watched, with eyes bulging. They watched
Mackay and Flood and the swarming Cornish and
Irish miners dig ahead slowly along a vein of silver
two inches wide. Two inches wide, four inches, ten
inches, one foot, ten feet, twenty feet, fifty feet,
three hundred feet wide! And they saw the Diedes-
heimer square sets on the same vein rising ten,
twenty, fifty, a hundred and fifty feet high! And
the length along the lode was a thousand feet, with
no end to it. Bonanza beyond the wildest dreams
of mining men!

And with this wealth, the West exploded. Nothing was too good. New York opera and fine hotels,
great bars and gambling rooms, oysters and cham-

pagne, velvet and brocades, jewels, silver bells for the churches, brass bands and rosewood pianos. Wagon trains toiled to bring the men of the mining camps everything for which their dollars were waiting. And after the wagons and stages came the railroads, narrow-gauge lines twisting and coiling up the heights of the Rockies or running ribbonlike into the desert. The West was raw and new. A group of miners decided that their favored saloon should have a chandelier, but one objected on the ground that no one knew "how to play it." Sandy Bowers and Eilley Orrum went to "Yoorup" to visit the Queen of England and to buy half of Paris from obliging Frenchmen. Pennies were refused by storekeepers in Idaho and nickels were gathered together as a nuisance and shipped to San Francisco. Youngsters running errands in the streets picked up twenty dollars a day in tips. Cannons boomed announcing presidential elections and holidays. The streets were a milling mass of ore wagons, horses, mules, burros, cursing teamsters, stagecoaches, and miners. "There was no night. . ." Saloons never closed and the hurdy-gurdy houses did a round-the-clock business.

But where the boom was rapid, the decline was equally so. Diamond City, located on Confederate Gulch in the Big Belt Mountains of Montana, came into being in 1865. Single pans of pay dirt yielded $1,000, and the total yield in its brief years of exis-

tence was $16,000,000 in gold. Within two years
the population soared to ten thousand persons, but
as the diggings were worked out, the miners and
assorted camp followers moved on. By 1870, the
"city" had 255 people, and a year later, 64. Today
there is nothing left. In the same state, two miners
found gold in 1869 on Cayuse Creek, a tributary of
Cedar Creek, near present-day Superior. Within a
year, ten thousand people had swarmed to these
diggings, but by 1871 the ore was exhausted. The
camp then moved upstream to newly discovered
Forest City. But by the winter of 1872, Forest City
collapsed in favor of Mayville, still farther up the
same creek. In two years Mayville also declined.
And the residents simply walked out of Mayville,
leaving behind them bar equipment, pianos, stoves,
billiard tables, and everything else which could not
easily be hauled away by pack train.

What was true of these towns was true also, to
greater or lesser degree, of all the mining camps,
and of their discoverers and owners as well. The
great Comstock Lode dropped in population from
40,000 to 100 persons, and has only recently crept
back to a meager thousand on the basis of its tourist
attractions and proximity to Reno and Lake Tahoe.
Comstock himself sold his original share in the
mines for $10,000, and later committed suicide in
Bozeman, Montana. The uproar and desert glories
of Tombstone are quiet, and the Bird Cage Theater

slumbers as a museum. Central City and its alert Opera Association cater to summer visitors and nostalgically revive the past during brief vacation weeks. Haw Tabor's wealth was dissipated and vanished utterly in the silver crash, while his beautiful wife, Baby Doe, froze to death, penniless, in the small cabin of the Matchless Mine. The fabulous Windsor, greatest hotel between Chicago and San Francisco, fell into disrepute on Denver's Larimer Street. Deserted Aspen has been turned into a ski resort.

But even though the story runs in a consistently tragic pattern, the memories of the boom days cannot be downed in the minds of old-timers. They remember the great days, the days of their own youth and the youth of the towns. And the hold which the early camps has upon the memories of men is nowhere more succinctly or aptly stated than in Joseph T. Goodman's poem on Virginia City, a Western classic which might have been written of any of the mining towns in New Mexico, Arizona, Montana, Idaho, Utah, or Colorado:

> In youth, when I did love, did love
>   (To quote the sexton's homely ditty),
> I lived six thousand feet above
>   Sea-level, in Virginia City;
> The site was bleak, the houses small,
>   The narrow streets unpaved and slanting,
> But now it seems to me of all
>   The spots on earth the most enchanting.

Let Art with all its cunning strive,
　Let Nature lavish all her splendor,
One touch of sentiment will give
　A charm more beautiful and tender;
And so that town, howe'er uncouth
　　To others who have chanced to go there,
Enshrines the ashes of my youth,
　And there is Fairyland, or nowhere.

Who tends its marts, who treads its ways
　Are mysteries beyond my guessing;
To me the forms of other days
　Are still about its centers pressing:
I know that loving lips are cold,
　And true hearts stilled—ah, more the pity!
But in my fancy they yet hold
　Their empire in Virginia City.

Unhallowed flames have swept away
　The structures in which I delighted,
The streets are grass-grown, and decay
　Has left the sunny slopes benighted—
But not for me: to my dimmed sight
　The town is always like the olden,
As to the captive Israelite
　Shone aye Jerusalem the Golden.

I would not wish to see it now,
　I choose to know it as I then did,
With glorious light upon its brow,
　And all its features bright and splendid;
Nor would I like that it should see
　Me, gray and stooped, a mark for pity,
And learn that time had dealt with me
　As hard as with Virginia City.

And, lest anyone feel that Goodman—speaking for any other Comstocker, miner, or for himself alone—exaggerated his feelings of sentiment for his beloved camp, let him read his separate, briefer poem which has the depth of prayer:

> If when we've done with earthly strife
>   There be a Paradise or Sheol,
> Or any other named abode
>   Which we may gain through love or pity,
> Grant me a heavenly Comstock Lode,
>   A spiritual Virginia City.

E ARLY whisky in the frontier West was rightly
named—Tangle-Leg, Forty Rod, Tarantula Juice,
Rookus Juice, Bug Juice, Lightning, and, more spe-
cifically, Taos Lightning. They were villainous
compounds, made from barrels of the vilest alco-
hol, with the addition of burnt sugar and various
flavoring extracts, not excluding a chaw of tobacco.
And guaranteed to maim or kill. Taos Lightning
struck a man on the spot, Tarantula Juice poisoned

him, Tangle-Leg left him weaving from one side of a dusty street to the other, and one drink of Forty Rod brought a man to his knees at precisely forty rods from the bottle. Utah's Valley Tan, made in the wild Henry Mountains, was only a poetic euphemism for equally murderous liquor. Small wonder that early cowboys, after a few snorts, howled that they had been suckled by grizzlies and raised with rattlesnakes; and that the shooting up of saloons and the gunplay of the streets naturally followed, to end frequently in death. Any man was a bad man with a load of the liquor, and its best recommendation was that it knocked men out before they could move into action.

The first saloons were simply stands by the side of the trail, upended barrels with a board across them and crude signs advertising Bar, Saloon, and Whisky. One pioneer entrepreneur in Idaho hauled his whisky until both he and his beasts were worn out. With a to-hell-with-it and this-is-as-good-a-place-as-any attitude, he set up shop at the point of collapse and a town grew around him. In Arizona and New Mexico, crude wickiups, open at all four sides, sheltered drinkers from the sun. Hastily constructed tents, shacks, and cabins housing whisky barrels and a plank bar were usually the first buildings in camp, the only evidence of advancing civilization. They were often "hotels" at the same time, since there was no other place to go, and the miner was offered the dubious two-bit privilege of sleeping on the beaten dirt or plank floor after drinking.

With the growth of the camps, however, the Western saloons as they are traditionally known today came into being. They are distinguished from others by a long bar with plenty of open space for the circulation of customers—miners, cowboys, dance-hall girls—and space for the gambling games, ranged against the wall facing the bar.

Latourette's Saloon, on Washington Street at Tin Cup, was physically representative. The interior was eighty feet long and thirty feet wide, and the Brunswicke-Balke-Callander bar itself was fifty feet in length. The saloon had a more pretentious entrance than most, with a double set of swinging doors, the outer doors of frosted glass and the inner set of latticework. The long bar was on the right-hand side of the saloon and on the left, from the entrance to the back, the gambling games were, in order, poker, dice, roulette, and faro. At the rear of the saloon an extension provided another room for private games of chance where the limits and bets were set by agreement of those playing. Latourette's, like many of the mining-camp saloons, had a second floor, the stairs running up from the far end of the bar, where there was a fine dining room managed by a French chef. Foods of all kinds, including a half lobster at $1.50, were served to the men of the town, whose population in the heyday of the '70's was 3,000. Also on the second floor and beyond the restaurant, at the front of the building, were two smaller rooms where "snap" games were run, the house taking a percentage of the winnings from the dealer, who put up his own money.

The bar and back bar of the saloons were usually of Brunswicke-Balke-Callander manufacture, of walnut or mahogany, and the pool tables, cues, billiard balls, and poker checks were supplied by the same company. The firm also made the large racks to hold the heavy barrels of whisky, and the bar barrels were so evenly balanced upon these that even a child could pour a drink from a fifty-gallon keg.

The saloons handled three grades of barrel whisky, the quality dependent upon the age of ripening in charred oak kegs. Joe Gideon whisky was one of the best-known brands of the day; it was purveyed to miners by the drink or in flask bottles, wide at the top and tapering toward the bottom, and made flat to fit the hip. These bottles, hand-blown, are now collectors' items, particularly those which have weathered the desert sun and become as iridescent as the Roman glass of Mesopotamia. In addition to whisky dispensed and the opportunity for games of chance, the bars were equipped with pool and billard tables and supplied with all the reading matter in camp. A miner was welcome to sit all day at a table and read a month's supply of newspapers, to warm himself at the stove in winter, to sit and talk with friends at any time—with no compulsion to buy even a single drink.

The saloons were, and still are, essentially clubs, the social center of all mining camps and cattle towns. But let there be no condescension and talk about the "poor man's club." Men met there on an equal basis, millionaires and prospectors, cattle barons and cowboys, a custom which is still honored. Whisky was sold to all comers at the same price, the third or fourth drink was traditionally on the house, and Joe was as good as Bill, with no "Misters" in the place. As the men stood at the bar, an outsider could no more tell the cowboy working for his monthly wage from the cattleman owning fifty thousand head than he could tell the mine owner from the four-dollar driller. Neither by their clothes, their manners, the subject of their conversation, nor their speech. The frontier social club, the saloon, was the greatest single influence in the melting pot of the West. Here men learned of each other and the country. Here they transacted their business and told their tales. Here their humor was sharpened and their disasters ignored. Here they became Americans, whatever their Scottish, Cornish, Italian, German, or Irish origins may have been. And today even the governors of Western states, if they are wise, enter the saloons simply—

without putting on airs or "front"—because here
one man is the equal of another, and Western democracy judges clearly and works swiftly.

The decoration of the saloons, haphazard, unself-
conscious, reflected a man's club, and the saloons
now surviving from the last century are museums
in themselves. There are the gaudy ladies, stark
naked or coyly involved with a fan, decorating
calendars in the less pretentious bars, and, in the
once wealthy hotels, displaying their nudity in oils.
In the Windsor Hotel bar there is a classic nude being transported toward Olympian heights by a
Grecian god; and the bartender will, on request,
press a rubber bulb under the bar which carries
a stream of air back of the canvas to the vicinity of
her navel, causing the damsel to palpitate ecstati-
cally and the customer to order another cooling
round. On the more masculine side are the widely
favored Anheuser-Busch pictures of Custer's Last
Stand, and the current Acme beer still life of
broken wagon wheel, six-shooter, spurs, gold pan,
and nuggets. All the bars in the Western states are
decorated with moose, elk, antelope, or deer heads,
game shot by the owner of the bar or by his customers. In the mining camps, there are cases of ore
specimens, not consciously gathered for display,
but simply chucked helter-skelter in the glass case
as samples of ore in the region and to settle argu-
ments—gold-bearing rose quartz, green copper, sil-

ver. There are samples of what were once twelve-
by-twelve mine timbers, crushed by the weight of
the earth to a narrow three inches, heavy as iron;
smooth lengths of diamond drills, the ore core
showing bonanza or borrasca in the rock beyond
the mine face; gilt-edged stocks, now worthless, but
once the talk of all miners; canceled checks drawn
to names famous in Western history; old picks,
miners' lanterns, shovels, and other equipment
gnawed and rusted by the earth. There are early
prints, Currier and Ives, lithographs, wood engravings, local paintings, and American primitives that
gather dust over poker tables and set the collector's
mouth to watering. "Sell them? Hell, no, they're
part of the place . . . been here a long time." There
are crystal chandeliers, beveled mirrors, rare bar
glasses, antique jukeboxes with sixteen-inch, flex-
ible copper discs, and old lamps with great globes,
some of them deeply colored a non-Victorian and
double-standard red. In the cow country, the bars
are adorned with guns, spurs, sombreros, iron cattle brands, riatas, and leather work. The guns and
spurs are identified. "That there belonged to
Johnny-behind-the-Deuce." And the sombrero may
have a bullet hole through it, stained with old
blood. Burnt into the walls and beams of the room
are the brands of the state—as at Elko and Willcox
—and photographs and drawings of cowboys, ro-

deos, ranches, and prize cattle hang proudly over the bar.

The names of the saloons are no less colorful than their physical trappings. There were Buckets of Blood over the whole West, but the two famous ones remaining are on Park Street in Livingston, Montana, and on C Street in Virginia City, Nevada. The Livingston Bucket of Blood was the center of a roaring, rough district where Tex Rickard, Kid Brown, and Soapy Smith operated a gambling house before heading north with the Alaska rush. Madame Bulldog ran a saloon—so-called—in the same district. She weighed one hundred and ninety pounds stripped—and legend has it that not infrequently she was—and acted as her own bouncer. Calamity Jane was her associate for a time, but there came a parting of the ways when Calamity found herself propelled through the swinging doors. Did Calamity fight back? "Calamity was tougher'n hell, but she wasn't crazy!"

The Comstock Bucket of Blood carries its name's tradition outside the saloon itself to an old-fashioned, windowed hearse, or "gut wagon," upon which tourists clamber macabrely to be photographed, and also peddles a current ballad intituled "Who Shot Maggie in the Freckle?"

> Who shot Maggie in the freckle,
> Who shot Maggie on the Divide,

Who shot Maggie near Gold Hill
And ran away to hide?

Maggie was my boyhood sweetheart,
She loved me in the town on the hill,
And she never showed her freckle
To anyone but me, her Bill.

But she must have let someone see it,
Because there isn't any freckle any more;
The Johnny who shot her in the freckle
Made a perfect bull's eye score.

And now Maggie lies a-dying,
And she'll be dead in a day or two,
And she keeps on plaintively saying,
"Bill, my freckle belonged to you.

"And I wouldn't let anyone see it,
Nobody but you, my Bill;
If you catch the Johnny who shot me,
Hang him high on the Geiger Hill.

"And the reason that he shot me,
Shot me so harshly through and through,
Is because I was saving my freckle,
Just for you, my Bill, just for you."

Now I'm going to be sad and lonely
When Maggie passes away,
And I'm going to miss Maggie's freckle
Every single day.

So tell me all you muckers,
All you hardrock drillers, too,
Tell me the truth very quickly
And don't let me be blue,

Who shot Maggie in the freckle,
Who shot Maggie on the Divide,
Who shot Maggie near Gold Hill
And ran away to hide?

There were Silver Dollar Clubs and Gold Coin saloons throughout the region, and various Palace, Oriental, Pastime, Eldorado, and Ophir bars. Some were named with distinctive reason. The "62" was so called because the elaborate bar, inset with mirrors at knee level, had been shipped around the Horn in 1862. The Crystal Bar was justly proud of its costly and identifying chandeliers. The Sawdust Corner still makes a fetish of inch-deep sawdust, and the Smokery-Delta Saloon of necessity combined its original cigar sign of the Smokery Club with the salvaged, frosted Delta doors of an earlier saloon to create its hyphenated name. There was an Eye Opener Saloon, and a bluntly realistic Road to Ruin, with a bald invitation scrawled under its sign—Come In And Die. Some saloons simply took their names from the color of their painted fronts —The Red Front and The Silver Front. In La Junta, Colorado, The Blue Front catered to cowboys, advertising:

Range: The Old Blue Front.
Brand: The best brands of whisky that all cattlemen desire.
Earmarks: Frostbitten.

The standard drink in the western saloon was whisky, whisky straight. It was not served by measure into a shot glass, but drawn directly into a man-sized tumbler from the barrel; or, as bottled whisky and brand whisky became available, the bottle itself was set before the customers. The bartender—the "professor" or "doctor"—charged the drinkers by gauging the whisky remaining in the bottle against what he had first set up. There were no fancy drinks to begin with, but as the camps grew, everything from cocktails to imported liqueurs were to be had. One of the favorite early combinations was the Mule Skinner's cocktail, a rough combination of blackberry brandy and barrel whisky, famous in Colorado. To Butte goes the credit for inventing the Shawn O'Farrell, now nationally known by the debased term of "boilermaker." There was nothing fancy about a Shawn O'Farrell. It was, and is, simply a glass of whisky followed by a glass of beer, and, selling for ten cents, was the daily stand-by for miners when they came off shift. The whisky cut the dust and the beer quenched the thirst. Bill Burke, who shares with Joe Duffy the honor of being Butte's poet laureate, praises the drink in a poem ending:

> Oh, yes, they boast of lordly liquors
> Brought from corners of the earth,
> Creme-de-minthe and Parisian absinthe
> And high-toned beverages of worth.

But I'd stake my bottom dollar,
Also my honor and repute,
On the humble Shawn O'Farrell
Sold at quittin' time in Butte.

It was a custom, now honored only in the going camps, for the house to buy the first drink for the miner when he came off shift. The miner needed only to place his empty lunch bucket on the bar, and there beside it would be his "usual." The custom applied also to the first drink of the day in any given bar, whether morning, noon, or night. Even as late as ten years ago on the Comstock, a resident in good standing could walk the length of the main street, stopping at each of the sixteen bars, and have his "first" on each house, returning during the day —or the next days—to buy back.

There were other customs as well, and the Johnny-Come-Lately should be aware of them, certainly those still in force. For one, it is extremely bad form—even a heinous social crime—to drink alone. No bartender or customer will hint, much less insist, that anyone at the bar buy a drink for another person. But if a person stands drinking alone, he is apt to be left alone. No questions are asked and he can nurse his beer in peaceful solitude, if that is what he wants. But if he wants to move into the spirit of the town, learn its traditions, hear tales of its past, it behooves him to make friends by at least offering to buy the bartender a round. Whisky on the bar is like bread upon the waters: no self-respecting Westerner will accept a drink from another without offering to buy back. And if he does not have the money to buy back, he will clearly say so before accepting an offered drink. It goes without saying, of course, that to refuse a drink even from a total stranger—without apologies as adequate as "ulsters"—is a direct and unforgiveable insult. Men were killed for less on the old frontier.

There are still other customs. Where a man has won considerable at gambling in a saloon, he will, if a good sport, offer to buy the boys a drink, certainly those who have been near him at the blackjack or poker tables. The same holds true of the slot machines in the smaller saloons, a point of etiquette which is a stumbling block for many tourists and visitors. If a person hits the jackpot on a machine, local custom is to buy the bartender a drink and at least make a gesture toward including others at the bar. The machine should also be taken off "pay," and the winning bells, plums, or jackpot symbols spun off so that the next player has an even break and does not have to waste a coin to put the machine in circulation again. It was the break given to the first player; he, in turn, should give it to the next. Where a slot machine with a winning combination stares a player in the face, it has, ninety-nine times out of a hundred, been played by a tourist who does not know local custom. There is nothing so infuriating to residents as the tourist who enters a bar, plays two coins, wins the jackpot, and leaves without having bought a drink or taken the machine off pay. He is fervently damned until he is out of the region. Had he taken the machine off pay and merely offered to buy a drink, he would at once have become *persona grata* rather than "a guy so stingy he'd chase a mouse to Hell for a punkin seed." This custom, of course, does not apply to the big gaming places in Reno and Las Vegas, but to the smaller ones which are essentially saloons and clubs rather than gambling houses.

With the saloons serving him as clubs, with the privilege of running a tab or chit on the bar for as long a period as a month, it is small wonder that the Westerner should drink well and drink more heavily. And the casual manner in which whisky has always been accepted is enshrined in a story widely current in the West and told of every camp from the Mexican border to the Canadian line:

Two miners, standing on the boardwalk of their booming camp, eyed with satisfaction a string of eleven mules bringing in supplies. The first ten mules packed two kegs of whisky apiece, and the miners were high in their praise of the sensible merchant importing this necessity. They turned their attention then, with open-mouthed astonishment, to the eleventh mule, also burdened. "Now what in hell does he think we're going to do with all that flour!"

GAMBLING was as casual and natural to the old West as a drink of whisky and as easy to come by. The "gentlemen of the sporting fraternity"—never gamblers—were ready to accommodate miners and cowboys with all known games from faro to chuck-a-luck, poker to dice, panguingui to three-card monte. And when professional dealers were not on tap, the men played their own hands of stud or blackjack, sitting in the bunkhouse after work or studying the cards around the green baize tables of the local saloons.

The singlehanded shuffling of silver dollars, the slap of the deck, the click of checks tossed into the pot, the whirring roll of the roulette wheel—all were sounds pervading each saloon of the West. The *rien ne va plus* of France became the blunt "Game!" and the commanding "Bets!" replaced the softer *faites vos jeux, messieurs*. Dust and nuggets, gold and silver dollars—hard money that a man could feel—changed hands across the table. In big games, men bet their cattle and ranches and mines. And the biggest bet ever wagered was the whole Territory of New Mexico, signed away by the Governor—albeit at pistol point—and tossed in as a "raise" against a Texas gambler who had bet ten thousand head of cattle and his ranch, but who couldn't "call" against the Territory.

In the mining camps and cow towns, there were no gambling "hells," no places, that is, devoted exclusively to the business of gambling. As at Latourette's Saloon in Tin Cup, each bar had its own equipment, at least two or three tables given over to some game of chance. Whenever a man entered his "club," whenever he stopped for a drink, the opportunity to play was at hand. At the saloons in the smaller communities, the bets were not high as a general rule, nor are they today. The players were content to limit themselves to two-bit, half-dollar and dollar bets, setting a limit for themselves also on their losses. They rolled "razzle-dazzle" and "captain and the crew" from the leather dice cups for their drinks and cigars at the bar, paying double or nothing.

But in the boom towns and in the larger cities—Denver, Santa Fe, Albuquerque—there was heavier play, and here gambling establishments flourished. The bar was incidental—as it is today at the big Reno and Las Vegas clubs—and the games were the central attraction. At the famed Texas House in Leadville, Clint Roudebush played with twenty-five dollar chips, and one hundred thousand dollars changed hands here in a single night. The doors were never closed, and the dealers worked around the clock in eight-hour shifts. The Board of Trade Saloon and the California Concert Hall were equally popular. At the Gentry & Crittenden House in Virginia City, Nevada, Joe Timberlake, an Arizona rancher, played one-thousand-dollar chips at faro and lost forty-two thousand dollars in a brief spree. "At the Santa Fe hotel, enormous piles of silver weighed down the tables, and frequently ten thousand dollars changed hands in ten minutes. Businessmen would publicly lose or win a thousand dollars with the greatest nonchalance." In Denver there were the Leadville Club, the Arcade, the Capitol Club, the Cates Club, and the Jockey Club. Unnumbered thousands of dollars were won and lost here annually, and for a single player to lose ten or fifteen thousand in an evening was not unusual. Infrequently, he might win as much—infrequently, because the great majority of the games were crooked, operated by gamblers who were as dexterous and unscrupulous as Soapy Smith.

Jefferson Randolph Smith bossed the roughs of Denver, ruled the town of Creede, and sold soap. The quality of the soap was poor, the cake was small, and it cost five dollars, but because Soapy wrapped twenty, fifty, and hundred-dollar bills inside the paper cover of some pieces, the suckers flocked to his street stand and happily purchased. No one ever won. Smith's shills and confederates were the lucky "winners" who returned the money to Soapy after the show. Where he was quick-fingered at wrapping, juggling, and picking the proper pieces of soap from his basket, Soapy was equally gifted at the shell game, three-card monte —"The hand is quicker than the eye, gentlemen; pick the ace"—and at manipulating the deck. Soapy followed money wherever it was to be found, and his searches led him to the Klondike rush and the town of Skagway, where he met his death at the hands of vigilantes, his trigger finger having been as nimble as his card dealing.

Where Soapy had his specialty, other gamblers had theirs. One enterprising dealer, Manuel Blasos —known as Old Blazes—toured New Mexico with a "hell on wheels" in 1883. As brightly decorated as a circus bandwagon, his carriage, fixed up with roulette, faro, and dice games, and with three windows cut into each side, was drawn by six plumed horses. They conveyed his establishment wherever the pickings seemed good, to local fairs and mining strikes, crossroads and out-of-the-way towns.

Women dealers were soon introduced into the gambling houses, not because they were more adept at the games, but simply to display them to women-hungry men who were attracted by them and minded their losings the less. A visitor to Nevada in 1861 wrote:

"Women of very questionable character preside at the tables, and the unwary and susceptible, dazzled by the glittering ore which lies in compact piles on the tables, and the charms of the presiding Amazons, are soon engaged in assisting to increase the dimensions of these heaps. Oh, it is horrible to contemplate such proceedings. Last night I saw an exceedingly well-dressed young man enter an establishment, and, prompted by curiosity, I determined to do likewise in order to watch him. Presently he seated himself opposite one of these bewitching creatures and pulled from his pocket sixty dollars in gold. In a few moments it was gone, when, nothing daunted, he went still farther into his pocket, and laid sixty more before the eager eye of the fair dealer. Of course it was soon lost. He was then upon the point of leaving, when the by-standers sneered at his "pluck," which impelled him to try his luck again. Pulling one hundred dollars from his pocket, he foolishly bet it—and lost!"

Of the gambling games in the West, faro was by all odds the most popular. It had come to the West from France by way of New Orleans and the Mississippi. Its "tiger" beckoned all men, and most accepted the challenge to fight. Faro derived its name from the French *Pharaon,* whose picture decorated the cards in France, and it acquired the "tiger" from the Bengal tiger which adorned the chips and the layout in America. Usually there also hung a painting of a tiger, or of a tigress and her cubs, in back of the game, so that the player could readily identify and find the tables. Faro was, fairly dealt, the game which afforded the customer almost an even break, with only a slight percentage in favor of the house. It is today legally played only in Nevada, and the curious may there kibitz the game at the Bank Club in Reno. The "lookout" still sits in his elevated chair watching the players and the dealer, noting the bets on the layout and the fall of the cards from the deal box. It is his responsibility to correct errors and arbitrate disputes. Chinese, cowboys, and miners—the old-timers of the West—sit quietly around the table, playing the cards to win or "coppering" their bets to lose, clicking off on the case-box abacus the cards which have passed out of play.

The cards were shuffled and placed face up in the deal box. The top card showing, the "soda," did not count in the play. Bets having been placed on the layout—consisting of the thirteen denominations from ace to king—the "soda" card was slipped off the top of the deck. The next card showing under it was a "loser" and counted for the bank, and the one succeeding the "loser" was a "winner" and counted for the player. The player, however, was allowed to play any card to win or lose, and he was paid off in even money, the amount of his bet. The last three cards were played as a unit, and the player guessing the correct order of their appearance, if they were of different denominations, was paid off at the rate of four to one. If two of these last cards were of the same denomination, the payoff was reduced to two to one. When two cards of the same denomination appeared during the play, prior to reaching the last three, it was termed a "split" and the house took half of the money wagered. Although there were ramifications permitting the player to parlay his bets, to split them among a group of cards, and to "string along," this was, in essence, the game of faro.

Where no two-card box, brace game, or other dishonest deal was involved, faro resolved itself to the simple matter of betting any card to win or lose, and—except for the splits—the player had virtually an even break. There was no thirty-six to one, with the added zero and double-zero, to buck as in roulette. It was even-Steven.

Small wonder that the game had its addicts, even though many of them lost.

A visitor in Denver in 1859 wrote, "I saw the probate judge of the county lose thirty Denver lots in less than ten minutes, at cards, in the Denver House on Sunday morning, and afterward observed the county sheriff pawning his revolver for twenty dollars to spend in betting at faro."

Parson Riley related that at Elko a gambler had come to him with a pitiful tale about his wife, culminating with his sobbing, "Oh, yes, my beautiful wife, my dearly beloved wife, has just died, and I have not a dollar to buy a coffin for her. I am a total stranger here and don't know what to do." Parson Riley stepped into the breach with, "The rose on the bush is beautiful, but the crushed rose in the hand is more fragrant. May this affliction make you to know the joyful sound of the gospel!" More tangible was a ten-dollar bill which he gave the man to help defray the cost of a coffin. Riley ended the account: "He left, profusely thanking me, and in ten minutes after he was gambling with it, and never was married at all."

A humorous poem, similar in content, survives from 1889 to describe another inveterate player:

'Twas midnight in the faro bank,
Faces pale and cheeks aglow,
A score of sports were gathered,
Watching fortune's ebb and flow.

There was one who saw the last turn
With eyes of deep dismay,
And, as the Queen slipped from the box,
Cried, "Broke!" and turned away.

For a moment on the table
Down his throbbing head he laid,
Then, looking round him wildly,
He clenched his hand and said:

"I'm a pretty slick young feller,
I've been given every deal,
Have often dropped my bankroll,
But was never known to squeal.

"But this evening I am weary,
And my socks are hanging low,
My usual gait is 2:13
But tonight I'm trotting slow.

" 'Tis not for myself I'm kicking,
I've a friend that's near and dear
Who is lying, worn with sickness,
A couple of blocks from here.

"She's my darling, gents, my darling,
But they say she's got to croak,
And the medicine to save her
I can't get—you see I'm broke."

"Here's a dollar," said the dealer.
A smile lit up his face,
"Thanks, old man,—damn the medicine,
I'll play it on the ace!"

As a rule, the old-time gamblers of the West were generous. "Like all men who gain money easily, they were openhanded and charitable. I never saw a place where more dollars could be obtained in less time for a helpless woman or orphan than among those gaming tables." So wrote Albert Richardson about Denver. In one afternoon at Creede, Soapy Smith collected enough money to build the first church. And Parson Riley, swindled out of his ten dollars, was surprised to see "a dozen or so of the fraternity" seated before him in front-row pews on a Sunday. "I supposed that they were coming after me for another funeral sermon. But no, the winner had to give the stake money, which was quite large, and his chums came along to see that he did it. When the box went around, a small sackful of gold and silver was emptied into it."

The tradition of wide-open gambling, thoroughly legalized, persists in Nevada. While faro is disappearing slowly, there remain the standard games of crap, roulette, blackjack, and poker. Slot machines—the one-armed bandits—are found everywhere, in restaurants, drugstores, gas stations. All hotels have gaming equipment and gambling rooms—the famous Stockmen's in Elko, the Arlington in Carson, the Riverside, the Golden, and the new Mapes in Reno, the palatial Last Frontier in Las Vegas, the Big Meadows at Lovelock. In them may be found something of the old West, not alone in the games themselves but in the players as well.

Where the tradition is at its liveliest, however, is in the big clubs of Reno and Las Vegas, the Bank, the Palace, Harrah's, the Boulder, and Harold's. Large as they all are, Harold's tops the heap. The establishment itself and all figures connected with it are fantastic. Its doors are never closed, and five thousand customers a day are clocked through them. Its two hundred and twenty slot machines— from nickels to silver dollars—roar day and night and sound like the rolling of a fast freight. The jackpot is hit on an average of once every minute. The Club spends fifty thousand dollars a year for playing cards alone. Sixty million match clips are purchased for free distribution every three years. Fourteen hundred highway billboards, from Maine to Texas and Florida to Oregon, boast "In Reno It's Harold's Club," "Harold's Club or Bust." Free license plates advertising the Club are given away at gas stations throughout Nevada. Large advertisements appear weekly in every newspaper in Nevada.

Indoors the Club claims the only escalator in Nevada, as the Crystal of the last century boasted the only chandeliers. The second-floor bar is inlaid

with two thousand silver dollars, and behind the
bar there is a whiskyfall, a three-foot cascade which
flows with Old Forester and from which the skep-
tic or the thirsty may sip from a dipper. In one
game room there is a plastic, life-sized covered
wagon. Paintings on glass, illuminated from behind, portray lynchings, shootings, holdups, and
other colorful events in Nevada's history. On the
second floor also, there is a wall-sized reproduction
of Lake Tahoe. Every half hour lightning and
thunder burst over the Lake, and rain pours over
miniature trees.

The Club's five hundred employees include permanent electricians and carpenters. A staff of fifteen does nothing but repair slot machines. The
Club's own detectives patrol the games. Hostesses
guide the visitor who comes merely to look, and
women dealers, wearing bolero jackets stitched
with "Harold's Club" and their own names, smile
over the blackjack tables or the roulette wheels.

Bets from five cents to a thousand dollars are
taken from all comers, and for the tourist who
has no wish to gamble there is a large souvenir
stand which does a thriving business selling me-
mentos of the Club and other items of current
Western Americana. In effect, Harold's Club is the
Macy's of gambling and, like Macy's, is leagues
ahead of its competitors both in volume and variety
of business. Millions of dollars cross its tables an-

nually, into the pockets of customers, into the coffers of the Club.

Harold Smith bought the business at the present location of the Club, at 326 North Virginia Street, for five hundred dollars in 1935. He had little more than an added five hundred dollars in his pocket to bank any games, so he started with what was literally penny gambling. Harold, who gave his name to the Club, put in his father, Raymond I. Smith, as manager and brains of the concern, and his brother, Raymond A. Smith, became secretary-treasurer. Their total equipment consisted of two decrepit slot machines and a penny roulette game operated by a common, kitchen-variety mouse. The mouse, released from a cardboard box at the center of the wheel, ran around the wheel to disappear into one of the thirty-eight possible holes. That number paid off, and the mouse was produced again to repeat his task.

The next development in the Club's progress was actually no step forward. To vary the game, the Smiths introduced Japanese white mice. "I didn't know it, but the little bastards are cannibals!" The proprietors woke every morning to find half their "dealers" minus legs and ears. Ray Smith then took a hard look at the roulette table and the two slot machines. "I decided that we'd been playing this thing wrong. I made two resolutions and we've stuck to them. The first was to run a gambling place where anyone could play for high or low stakes, just as they wanted. The second was to advertise the place fully, from hell to breakfast." And a third resolution, implicit in Harold's Club from the beginning, was to run the games honestly, not only as required and enforced by Nevada law, but as required and enforced by the Club itself.

To protect the players and the house as well, the Club goes to extraordinary lengths. In addition to a carefully selected detective force, the Club trains its own employees, preferring to hire the nonprofessional dealer rather than the professional. "One of the best crap dealers we've got was a schoolteacher in Pennsylvania." This selection and training of the staff makes it almost impossible for an outsider to make any crooked arrangement with a confederate who is dealing. As a further protection, the Club maintains its own statistical staff, and where a table shows unusual losses or winnings—beyond the percentage norm—it is at once closely watched for crooked dealing. The dice used at the Club are of special manufacture and each one carries its serial number. They are kept locked in the Club's vaults until needed for play, and no dealer knows in advance the serial numbers which he will receive, so that there is no possibility that either a dealer or a customer can switch to dice which have been prepared with a corresponding number. Lastly, the Club keeps a blacklist of all known crooked dealers and none is hired. "Our policy is to give the customer as good a play as possible. The percentage of the games is enough for the house."

While the Club protects the customer and does everything in its power to protect itself, it nevertheless loses a certain amount annually to the crooked gambler. "I estimate that we get taken for $100,000 a year." How? "Why, they crimp cards, sandpaper them, mark them with their fingernails, punch pin marks into them with a pin concealed in a bandaged finger, hold them out, and do everything else to cheat us. They bring their own dice and switch on the game, play Greek shots, and then have the nerve to squawk when we show them the door." The Club has controlled the dice problem, but the cards are more difficult. Where a dealer suspects a customer of crooked play, however, the player is "old decked" out of the game. With every few hands, a new deck is cut open, so that the player marking the cards has no chance to profit from his markings before a new deck is substituted in play.

Aware of the gambling instinct and that weakness of human nature which impels a man to play beyond his means, Ray Smith boldly warns all players never to play any amount which they cannot afford to risk. "You can win at gambling, but you can't beat the game." There is not a single sign in the Club which urges customers to patronize the tables. On the contrary, every cartoon and sketch on the walls of the ground floor urges the customer *not* to play. And, further, there are no come-on players or shills in the Club.

Beyond the inherent and unchangeable percentage which favors the Club in each game, it is as honestly operated a gaming house as has perhaps existed in the world—and immensely more profitable for the Harold's Club Smiths than anything which a Soapy namesake ever dreamed of.

W HILE their saloons provided entertainment
in the basic forms of whisky and gambling, the
men, nevertheless, out of boredom or from sheer
excess of animal spirits, turned their idle hours to
other forms of amusement and general hell-raising.
The cowboys who had spent months on the range,
like the sailor home from sea, turned out to paint
the town red. Their approach was one either of
war-whooping directness or of ambling innocence.

96

Their arrival, with jingling spurs and purses, was welcomed, and their hungover departure hastened.

Because the towns were so remote, and their populations so essentially clannish in terms of their own experience of cattle or mining life, the men's amusements were rough and, to the outsider, alarming and dangerous. Often enough, the outsider himself was the subject of entertainment. The Westerner's traditional scorn of the tenderfoot frequently assumed the active form of the original hotfoot, with shots accurately placed around the visitor's dancing feet. One unfortunate in Leadville had a can tied by a string to his coat tails. When told to "Git!", he got, and the miners fired at the can as he hightailed it down the street. Plug hats were tossed into the air for target practice. Cowboys invariably reserved the roughest horses for newly arrived greenhorns, and "dudes" were entertained by being forced to drink tumblerfuls of raw, frontier whisky. The "dude" was easily distinguished by his dress and language, was often an Easterner from Boston, Philadelphia, or New York, or a touring Englishman, or was sometimes a remittance man, wearing a monocle, spats, cane, and top hat. In addition to his outlandish and impractical costume, he was ignorant of the customs of the country, staring bug-eyed at gun-carrying cowboys, gambling tables, saloons, miners, and women of the town. He was too inquisitive, asking impertinent questions in a land and at a time when a man's business was his own and questioners were apt to be forcibly discouraged. He adapted himself to the ways of the land with difficulty, and his schooling in the West was often hard.

When a St. Louis drummer put on airs in a New Mexico town, preferring to eat alone in his hotel room rather than with the common folk, he was promptly arrested and clapped in jail on a charge of horse stealing. His case was argued seriously in court, the prosecution demanding that he be hanged forthwith. The defense attorney, assigned by the court, pled for the "culprit's" life. "How can anyone believe that this kindly gentleman, this upright drummer, this solid citizen, this fine businessman . . .?" And with every "this," the defense attorney came down with a resounding, open-palmed thwack on the bald head of the "kindly gentleman" until his crown resembled a shining red beet. The judge, summing up the case, began seriously enough, but after two minutes of haranguing burst forth with a belly-splitting laugh, and ran screaming with laughter from the court, followed by jury, attorneys, and witnesses. The dazed drummer, freed from the halter, learned at least not to snub his equals on the frontier.

Similarly, a greenhorn in Gayleyville, who had heard much of the shooting West, found that Curley Bill, leader of a rough band of cowboys, was

relatively friendly. The greenhorn should not, however, have confused barroom friendship with famil-
iarity. He made the error of boasting about town
that he was a member of Curley Bill's gang and
that other cowboys were, in consequence, afraid
of him. Curley Bill heard of it and invited him to
drink at one of the saloons, an invitation which the
"dude" accepted with alacrity. Once indoors, the
newcomer found himself dancing to the tune of six-
shooters, his hat riddled with bullets and his pockets
emptied over the bar for refreshments for the
crowd. He left town suddenly, subdued and wiser.

Without malice or educational purpose, the men
played scarifying hoaxes on other greenhorns. One
such was informed, with appropriate secrecy, of a
freshly buried corpse, heavy not only with the
dead weight of death, but weighed down also with
valuable jewelry, rich rings, a thick watch, and a
chain of twenty-dollar gold pieces. While the in-
formant stood guard, the greenhorn was persuaded
to work mightily in the night to disinter the body
for its loot. At the point where he was tired, thirsty,
and close to exhaustion from his labor, shouts of
"Ghoul!" and "Grave robber!" and the sound of
heavy forty-fives and blasting shotguns galvanized
him into precipitate, pell-mell flight. When, after
long waiting and quaking in the bush, he wearily
crept back to town, he overheard much angry talk
of lynching a certain grave robber, if he could be

located. "We'd string him up!" The tenderfoot professed full agreement. He was then allowed to drink at the bar with the others—on the money found in the grave robber's coat, left behind at the scene of the "crime."

A like joke was played on another newcomer in Creede, a salesman, who looked forward eagerly to visiting, with a local friend, the two blonde and beauteous daughters of Old Man McClintock, reputedly a devil with a gun in defense of virtue, but coincidentally out of town on the evening in question. Armed with bottles of whisky, the local citizen and the salesman climbed the hillside to McClintock's cabin where, instead of inviting damsels, they were met with a charge of buckshot. The "friend" cried out that he was shot, and the salesman plunged, rolled, and tumbled down the hillside to the nearest saloon, where he gave an account of the terrible shooting. Instead of a sympathetic and excited audience, however, the salesman was horrified to find his listeners looking at him with suspicion. "You mean Joe was shot and you left him up there to die alone?" "Anyone knows McClintock hasn't got two daughters." "You wouldn't have shot Joe yourself, would you now?" While Old Man McClintock, Joe, and others drank the salesman's whisky in the hillside cabin, the salesman himself sweated and trembled under the mounting accusations in the saloon. At last, inching toward the door, a providential opportunity came for him to "escape." He bolted down the main street and out of town, a few scattered shots urging him on his way. He was never seen again in Creede.

Among themselves, the cowboys raised virtually every kind of hell imaginable. They and their horses were inseparable, and they rode them precisely where neither God, man, nor beast had ever intended that they should ride. They spurred them into the big saloons for a drink from the saddle, rode them to the card tables for a quick hand of poker, and played a wild game of billiards from horseback. They even invented a game of "pool polo" with their mounts, turning a single, cavorting horse around on the pool table until the last ball had been pocketed by the horse's hoofs. In Montana, two cowboys terrified staid passengers on a Northern Pacific train by riding their horses through the dining car. And at Missoula, a cowboy wagered that he could ride his horse into every room of Sam Arthur's hotel, and would have and could have if he had not been stopped by fourteen bullets from the outraged proprietor.

Their other amusements were rough. Leadville, which was one of the wildest towns of the West in the '80's, humorously reported a leap-year dance: "Leadville has had a leap-year ball which was conducted in proper style. The girls had three knife fights and then a general shooting affray, while

the men huddled together in a corner and yelled."
In Elko, Nevada, a madame of the "line" wagered
that she could walk three times around town as
naked as Godiva and that no one would bother
her. Soldiers from a nearby fort entered into the
spirit of the occasion and guaranteed her an audience by preceding her with a full band. In Virginia
City, another "lady," watching foot races from a
window on C Street, shouted that she could beat
all entrants. Bets were placed and, at the moment
of the starting gun, she sprinted unclothed and
barefooted from the doorway, leaving the men staring after her. It would have been most ungenteel
of them to have chased her up the main street. She
won, hands down.

In Elko, after a wild and uproarious Saturday
night, the local paper reported that "the boys must
have had a big time yesterday evening—a squaw
was found hanging from the flagpole this morning." And where "amusements" of such nature existed, it was inevitable that the men should patronize the stronger and more bloodthirsty sports which
have since been outlawed. In Leadville, ordinary
boxing was varied by fighters who slugged it out on
top of a twenty-foot derrick, the loser receiving not
only punishing blows but the hazard of the fall.
Cripple Creek staged one of the very few bull fights
ever held in this country. In Butte, the fight was
varied by pitting a bear and a bull against each

other, each animal dying from gored or slashed wounds. Cockfighting was brought to the camps by Irish and Cornish miners. Dogfights were traditional, and enlivened on one occasion at Butte by setting two greyhounds and a bulldog against a wolf, the dogs winning easily. Brutal shin kicking and head butting contests were violent departures from classic rules of ring sport.

The glorious Fourth was celebrated with frontier abandon. Introduced with dynamite blasted from anvils or exploded in whole barrels on nearby hillsides, the day and night celebrations progressed from early-morning flag raisings to the utter fatigue of the Fifth. In a mining camp of any size, there was the usual parade of the National Guard in dress uniform and the various volunteer fire companies with gleaming equipment. The parade, with its bands, was followed by foot races of all description and by the spirited hose races of the fire companies, each company spurred on by its supporters who bet lavishly on their favorite. Next came the chief mining-camp contests, the rock drilling competition with prizes running into the thousands of dollars for the champion team—men who could pound the drill inches deep into hard granite in as many minutes—and by the mucking contest, the winner shoveling a huge pile of broken rock into empty ore carts. These contests were a matter not only of brawn but skill as well, and the winners

were honored by their community and often represented it in contests involving champion teams
from other camps. Even today, where the mechani-
cal drill has supplanted the doublejack, men still
compete in the traditional contest, swinging the
four- and eight-pound hammers with a steady, skill-
ful rhythm. The sound of steel striking steel that
bites into granite can be heard from Bisbee to Butte
and from Virginia City to Cripple Creek on their
holidays. It is a sound reminding men of the one-
time greatness of the camps, and their mining heritage.

Following the outdoor events, the citizenry
moved into the saloons, where enormous quantities
of whisky were downed in honor of life, liberty,
and the pursuit of happiness. Fiddlers and piano
players added to the general gaiety. Where no
women were on hand, the men danced with each
other, whirling violently and ungracefully about
the room, occasionally winding up head over tea-
kettle among the clanging spittoons. It was during
such celebrations that the men saw "side-hill
lancers," an animal half-bird and half-beast, with
two short legs on the uphill side and two long long
legs on the downhill side:

> You can hear the lancer going round and round,
> Chasing the miner on his spree,
> For only he can see
> This side-hill lancer in this country West.

He cannot catch him on the plain
If only he'd run down quick,
But round and round and round he goes,
So don't go on the hill. . . .

Many a miner went on the hill, however. Axel the carpenter, in a betwixt and between state, drove a rusty nail into his foot. His friends recommended a doctor at once. Axel waved them aside— "Never had a doctor in my life." He headed straight for the Bucket of Blood Saloon, bought two pints of Old Crow, took off his shoe, poured one pint into it and the other into himself, and sloshed around town until cured. On his final spree, he lay down in a snowbank and quietly froze to death. Many miners have waked to find that thoughtful friends had taken care of them in their drunkenness, putting them gently to bed in open graves, in coffins, and beside corpses. One miner, on the morning after, was horrified to wake and find himself in the pesthouse, his face pocked and dotted with smallpox delicately applied with paint and brush by fellow carousers.

Fred Hart, who was never accused of being a teetotaler, described a morning-after celebrant in his *Reese River Reveille:*

"He came up the street with an unsteady gait, his legs now and again acting contrary, one foot trying hard to cross the path of the other. At last he reached a railing that stood by an open cellar-way, and here was a haven of rest for his weary and Fourth-of-July-racked soul. He grasped the railing to steady himself; then gradually his head sank down on the rail, and there was a bending of the knee joints. Slowly, carefully, he slid down the cellar stairs; the bottom step was reached; one long-drawn sigh, ending in a deep bass snore, and, away from the gaze of men and the City Marshal, the tired soul was at rest—a rest so perfect that all the firecrackers on earth could not have recalled him to the scenes of unrest of the day after the Fourth. He was there this morning, lying on his back, with the bright sun shining on his upturned face, and several blue-bottle flies sipping the sweetness from his parted lips. Reader, that man was once a little boy, and went fishing on Sunday, and robbed orchards and birds' nests, just like many and many another innocent boy; and had it not been for the demon of whisky, he might have grown up to be a member of the Legislature."

There were other occasions than the Fourth for celebrating. The spring and fall festivals, traditionally observed by all peoples of the earth, appeared in the West with typical local trappings. The calf roundups of the spring and the beef roundups of the fall brought together from scattered ranches cowboys and "reps" who, for their own amusement and the honor of the brand, competed with each other in bulldogging, bronc riding, rop-

ing, and lassoing of running animals. The men
were inordinately proud of their mounts and their
equipment, often spending every penny earned for
saddle, bridle, spurs, sombreros, and chaps. The
outfits were made for the cowboy's use: the sombrero to keep off the sun and to scoop up water for
his horse; the chaps to protect his legs from mes-
quite and brush; the high-heeled boots to fit the
stirrup and to dig deeply into the ground; and his
neckerchief to cover his face against the smother-
ing dust of the herd. But in addition to their being
useful, the cowboy made them colorful as well. His
chaps were decorated with nickel and silver buttons
and leather laces, his neckerchief was a bright red
or yellow, his sombrero a white or dust-colored
Stetson, and his boots often intricately designed
with stitching and embossed leather work. His saddle was his great pride, and for it he might spend
several hundred hard-earned dollars.

It was wholly natural that, out of the working
roundups, the present-day rodeos developed. Not
only was the cowboy's dress colorful, but there was
the moving color and action of horses and cattle,
the bucking broncos and the wild Brahma bulls,
the running calves and the whirling lasso. The
small side bets which cowboys placed on each other
at the roundups evolved into the thousand-dollar
prizes offered at the rodeos. The breaking of broncs
grew into the careful selection of the wildest un-

tamed horses for the spectacular exhibitions of the rodeo ring. And the arrival at roundup time of a small group of riders from a neighboring ranch was pyramided into the gay, colorful parades held now in Cheyenne, Durango, Reno, Tucson, and Phoenix. Far removed from the working life of the ranch, the rodeos, with their professional cowboys and cowgirls, nevertheless bring briefly to the cities a touch of the splendor and excitement of the old West.

During the three- or four-day period, the many towns go to elaborate lengths to condition citizens and visitors alike to the fiesta spirit, requiring, on penalty of kangaroo court and public ridicule, that each person wear some article of apparel or adornment characteristic of the frontier West. A complete spirit of informality reigns, and copper-riveted Levi's and blue shirts replace dinner jackets and business suits at hotels, banks, and offices. There is a "Howdy, stranger" atmosphere engendered which is not merely temporary, but carries over throughout the rest of the year, contributing to the characteristic democracy of the West.

There were still other occasions for parades and celebrations, including the big annual stockyard celebration in Denver, the Festival of Mountain and Plain, various commemorative Admission Days when the young states joined the Union, the annual meetings of the many Stockmen's and Mining As-

sociations, and the varied fiestas throughout the
Southwest on saints' days and religious holidays.
The visitor will know of the more obvious ones,
those widely advertised and backed by Chambers of
Commerce, but he will do well—if he wishes to
learn the life of the region—to ferret out the smaller doings, because there the people meet simply,
without the fanfare of publicity and Hollywood-
esque shows. At the purely local fairs he will find
the working ranchers and cowboys, the farmers
and housewives and their children, the natural, un-
sophisticated way of American life. Instead of a
ten-dollar box seat and blaring loud-speakers announcing events, he will find himself perched on
a corral fence, his heels hooked over a lower rail
and the announcements coming to him from a
neighbor who knows each participant and horse.
From the Stinkingwater to the Ruidoso, and the Big
Sandy to the Gila, the small, unheralded rodeos
and fairs will teach him more of the land and its
honest gentry than he can learn from half a dozen
of the highly organized variety, exciting though
they are. And always there will be a bit of Western
yelling and helling.

T HE "ladies" of the West who followed the
gold and silver strikes brought with them the first
semblances of civilization. More often than not,
they were the first women in the camps, and their
jewels, perfumes, and rouges, sweeping skirts, gay
bonnets, and parasols made an instantaneous impression upon the appreciative audience of rough
miners and cowboys. Men who had never bothered
to shave, who rarely bathed or changed their shirts,

began to pay some attention to dress, and the camps became profitable places for barber, haberdasher, and dry-goods merchant. Champagne and fine wines were added to bar stocks, and dance-hall girls brought an atmosphere of relative gentility to saloons where killings had kept pace with the flow of rotgut. The respectable, eyebrow-raised sisters who followed after condemned them, but the "ladies" deserve full frontier credit for softening the rough camps and making the advent of later civilization the easier. Their heyday has gone, in the West as elsewhere, yet even today, in mining towns where the male population far outweighs its feminine counterpart, the "girls" are legally condoned and accepted.

They were the "girls," the "dance-hall girls," and the "hurdy-gurdy girls," "crib girls" and the girls of the "Red Light" and the "district." They were the "parlor-house girls" and the "parlor-house Madames," the elite whose jeweled finery brought envious stares from the less fortunate "Cyprians" and "nymphs of the pave." Lastly, they were the "girls of the line," the most widely used and commonest term for them in the West.

And the "lines" of the West were famous, from Denver's fabulous parlor houses on Holladay Street to little cabins perched precariously in Idaho gulches, from Reno's Stockade to Cripple Creek's Myers Avenue, from Butte's Galena Street and

Venus Alley to Leadville's State Street and Ely's row of unpretentious cottages. The line at Butte, following the closing of the Barbary Coast, boasted of being the largest in the country, with more than a thousand girls there at one time between 1904 and 1917. Similar lines, not as populous, existed in Salt Lake, Tucson, Helena, Phoenix, and Santa Fe.

The girls and madames were legend. There was Little Gertie the Gold Dollar, Highstep Jennie, Madame Bulldog, and Silver Heels. Lattice Porch was affluent enough to own a shaded veranda, and Rowdy Kate was in and out of the Tombstone jail so regularly that her permanent residence was in doubt. Pansy Brasier ran a house in Butte, and Blonde Marie imported girls from Paris, catering chiefly to wealthy cattlemen and mine owners in Arizona. Crazy Horse Lil made a name for herself in Bisbee's Brewery Gulch, where she not only operated a house profitably, but added to her income by arranging holdups of her customers. Timberline was tall, crippled Slanting Annie walked with a tilt, and Madame Featherlegs rode stride-saddle at her "hog ranch" at Rawhide Buttes, Wyoming, her long, red underwear flapping about her legs like chicken feathers.

The girls were openly introduced in the mining camps. Madame Mustache followed the gold strikes through Idaho, Montana, Nevada, and Arizona. She operated her parlor house efficiently and dealt on the side a lucrative game of 21. In Tombstone she periodically advertised her girls, sweeping into a saloon with them and delicately sipping a glass while the men became acquainted. New arrivals in Virginia City were driven in open carriages along the main street and then entertained at the bars by way of a debut. Julia Bulette rode daily along C Street in a lacquered brougham, the doors of which were decorated with a crest of four aces. Sallie Purple, Frankie Page, and Mollie May brought their girls into Pop Wyman's notorious resort in Leadville to drink, gamble, and dance—and to meet the boys.

The girls who operated independently, without the backing of madames and without the luxury of parlor houses, advertised and displayed their wares simply and directly. In the majority of camps, they ultimately lived in segregated districts where their little cabins or "cribs" were illuminated by red lamps and curtains and where, in lieu of any street numbers, their names were posted in the windows or glass doorfronts—Jackie, Billie, Jane, Caroline, and Suzie.

In Denver, the line was dominated by Mesdames Jennie Rogers, Mattie Silks, Blanche Brown, Jennie Holmes, and Ella Wellington. They supported, for their customers and for the trade, the publication of Denver's *Red Book*, a pocket-sized guide to the "pleasure resorts" and a frank thumb-nosing of the

Social Registers and Blue Books. They advertised parlor houses with "23 Rooms, 3 Parlors, 2 Ballrooms, and 15 Boarders." Minnie Hall had "20 Rooms and 20 Boarders"—somewhat more tenanted—and offered a "Mikado Parlor" to those interested in the mysteries of the Orient. A "Cordial Welcome to Strangers" was guaranteed, and the parlor houses served the "Finest Wines, Liquors, and Cigars" to gentlemen seeking relaxation.

When Denver's city fathers objected to the flagrant signs along the length of Holladay Street, the madames removed them—to replace them with none too euphemistic invitations, MEN TAKEN IN AND DONE FOR. The city fathers were successful in changing the not inaptly named Holladay Street —actually for Ben Holladay, pioneer stage owner— to the prosaic Market Street, not less apt but more bluntly mercantile. They were less successful when they passed an ordinance requiring all "nymphs" to wear yellow ribbons in their hair as a badge of profession, so that purer sisters might readily detect and avoid them. Jennie Rogers and Mattie Silks decided to co-operate. With a vengeance. The afternoon following the edict, every prostitute in Denver strolled and sauntered along Fifteenth Street, wearing not only yellow ribbons, but yellow dresses, yellow parasols, yellow stockings, and yellow shoes. The street was a mass of yellow! When genteel ladies objected to the presence of the girls in shops and restaurants, managers could only stand by helplessly. They wanted no lawsuits brought by the capable Jennie Rogers. Enforcement died a-borning.

The lines were, of course, subject to periodic waves of reform, and pronunciamentos similar to those of the Denver fathers were directed at them. When these attacks were of local origin, the "sinners" bowed their heads for a day and then rose refreshed and more hell-bent than ever. The amenities had been observed, and everyone was content. But when an attack was made by someone not a member of the community, that was a different matter again.

When Julian Street, the author, visited Cripple Creek and its Myers Avenue line in 1914, he unmercifully attacked the town in a subsequently published article, calling it hideous, dull, and a disgrace. Judging from the article, Street seems never to have lifted his eyes above the "cribs" and to have talked—reformer and tenderfoot fashion— only with Madame Leo, known also as Leo the Lion. Cripple Creek and all its citizenry hotly resented the attack, and did something about it. The name of Myers Avenue was changed to Julian Street.

Street also visited the Elko line, morbidly staying up late at night for the brief stop of the train. Descending the steps of the Pullman, he merely looked at the red lights twinkling in the darkness of the desert night, shuddered at imagined horrors, and returned to righteous sleep—to awaken the following morning in the comparative safety of California. Why he objected so strenuously to the lines of mining camps and cattle towns—whose villainies, while robust, never equaled those of the big cities—is explicable perhaps because he objected to frankness. The West was never hypocritical.

Had he stopped to talk with old-timers or with the girls themselves, he would have found much good where he saw only the bad. Jennie Rogers, during the panic of '93, supported a hundred destitute girls in respectable boardinghouses until she could send them home to their relatives. Thrown out of work, the girls had come to her for employment, but she would not accept them, nor would she permit any other madame to employ them. Silver Heels, a dance-hall girl at Alma and Buckskin Joe, refused to leave the camps when smallpox ravaged the towns. Other women were removed to the safety of Fairplay, but Silver Heels stayed of her own accord to nurse the miners, who remembered her generous acts by naming Mount Silver Heels for her. Years after the epidemic, a heavily veiled woman frequently visited the cemetery, and men speculated that it might be Silver Heels, whose beauty had been destroyed by the disease. Similarly, Julia Bulette saw that poor families on the Comstock received anonymous gifts of food and that ragged children were clothed. When men died in the mines, she was the first to contribute money and food for the widows.

Julia's, or Julie's, legend has grown so that she has become the symbol of the western "lady," and her reputation has spread among the girls so that they look upon her almost as a saint of the profession, a more contemporary Magdalen. Men say today, half believing it, that Julie was buried in a silver coffin, that four bands preceded her hearse to the graveyard, that a parlor car on the Virginia and Truckee Railroad was named for her at the time, and that in her lifetime she was fabulously weathy. That is folklore and legend and will not die, but it is not the truth. It is true, though, that one of the mines of the Comstock was named the Julia for her; that she was elected an honorary member of Virginia Engine Company No. 1—the highest social honor possible in Virginia City and the only woman ever so honored; that one band, eighteen carriages, and the marching men of the Engine Company escorted her body to Flowery Hill Cemetery; that the band played funeral dirges on the way to the grave and the rollicking "Girl I Left Behind Me" as the procession returned; and that, in spite of, as well as because of, her profession, she was loved and honored by the men of Storey County during her lifetime, and by the people of Nevada after her death.

At the time of her death, Julia Bulette was thirty-five years of age. Some claimed that she was French or Creole, but *The Territorial Enterprise* reported that she was a native of London and had come to the California camps via New Orleans in 1853, residing in various West Coast towns until 1863, when she followed the rush to the Comstock. She was dark-eyed, tall, slim, beautiful, but beyond mere physical beauty possessed the deeper feminine characteristics which endeared her to the men—generosity, compassion, sympathy, and understanding. Her personality as well as her wit and humor must have been vibrant and living to dominate Virginia City as she did.

Julia was no ordinary Cyprian. In addition to her own lacquered carriage—albeit with four aces —she acted the lady not only in dress but in manners. Her house at the corner of Union and D Streets, where she lived alone, was, of course, the scene of many an "entertainment," but she permitted no rough-housing such as went on in other cabins and houses. She offered the men good conversation, taught them to recognize fine wines and champagnes, and not infrequently served dinners distinguished by rare and unusual delicacies. When she went to the Opera House accompanied by Tom Peasley, "chief" of the boys and her favored lover, she went to her own loge, wearing, in summer, an opera hood of white silk and purple velvet and, in winter, a sable cape with sable muff and wristlets.

Julia was not so much the lady, however, that she could not enter into the boisterous spirit and frontier fun of the Comstock. When Nevada became a state in 1864, and when Governor Nye was welcomed to the town, she proposed and helped build a huge floral arch over the main street. And no holiday or parade was complete without Julia riding enthroned on the gleaming brass and silver engine of Company No. 1. When fires threatened the town, she was on hand with food and coffee for the fire fighters and, on occasion, even assisted at the pumps herself. When funds were being raised for the Sanitation Fund, forerunner of the Red Cross, Julia bid as spiritedly for Gridley's symbolic sack of flour as any mine owner. And in the very early days of the camp, when Virginia City was threatened with attack by the Paiutes, Julia chose to remain with the men to nurse them, rather than to seek safety with the other women in Carson.

It is small wonder that the men of the town worshipped her, and equally natural that the good ladies of the place detested her, looking upon her as a menace to their family way of life and as a rival for their husbands' affections.

On Sunday morning, January 20, 1867, Gertrude Holmes, a neighbor and woman of the D Street line, found Julia Bulette murdered. It was late then, eleven-thirty in the morning, and Gertrude Holmes had entered by the open back door to call Julia to a prearranged breakfast. A Chinese had been there before her to bring in wood and make the regular morning fire; he had left without disturbing Julia, thinking that she was asleep. And still earlier, at five o'clock in the morning, a newspaper carrier had heard a loud scream coming from the direction of Julia's house, but as he made his rounds and even delivered a paper at her door, he heard no more, nor did he see anything unusual. Dr. Bronson and Dr. Gaston, who examined the body at noon, testified that she had been dead some six or eight hours, so that the single scream heard by the newsboy was probably Julia's lone, unanswered cry for help when attacked by her murderer.

Julia's body was lying with the head in a normal position on the pillow, but her feet and legs protruded to one side from under the covers. The undersheet on both sides of the body looked quite smooth, evidence that no one had occupied the bed with her. Her clothes lay on the floor beside the bed, as though she had simply dropped them and stepped out of them. On her forehead and the side of her head were deep bruises, and splinters and chips of wood were found in her hair. She had evidently been struck first with a stick of wood, which was found later in the room, but, protected as she

was by her hair, the blows had been insufficient
to kill her and had served only to waken her. When
she screamed, the murderer, alarmed at her out-
cry, had seized her by the throat and completed
death by strangulation. He had then systematically
robbed the house and departed.

The murder was not committed because of sex,
but for robbery. To kill a woman on the frontier,
even in a crime of passion, was a heinous offense,
but premeditatedly to murder her while she lay
defenseless in bed and with robbery as the motive
was to place the doer of the deed utterly beyond
the pale. Had the man been caught at the time, he
undoubtedly would have received short shrift at
the hands of the outraged miners. As it was, he was
not to escape.

John Millain was the murderer, and it was later
discovered that he had been stupid, idiotic, auda-
cious, or ghoulish enough—the reader may take
his choice—to sit up with the corpse at the funeral
parlor on the night following the murder and also
to march in the funeral procession wearing crepe
on his arm. The main facts of that funeral procession have been noted, but an additional one rounds
out the full story. As the cortege, with band, carriages, and marching men, departed from the Engine Company's fire house on B Street, the good
ladies of the town closed their shutters and drew
their shades, fearful of observing their own hus-

bands in the line of march, and reproving the great
honor accorded to Julia Bulette.

The murderer was not caught at once. Several
innocent men were, of course, arrested but released
for lack of evidence and because of good alibis. It
was not until some three months later that Martha
Camp, a friend of Julia's, surprised a man carrying
a large knife in her room. The man, Millain, es-
caped at the time, but she recognized him several
days later on C Street and had him arrested on a
charge of attempted murder and robbery. While
he was confined in jail, evidence was brought forward, on May 23, 1867, that he was the murderer
of Julia Bulette. A Mrs. Cazentre of Gold Hill had
purchased a dress pattern from him for forty dollars, which had initially been sold to Julia by the
firm of Harry and Sam Rosener. Also, Millain had
sold to Nye, the jeweler, a diamond pin which was
known to have belonged to her. With these clues,
the police searched for Millain's possessions and
located a trunk which he had left with a French
baker on North D Street. When opened, the trunk
was found to be filled with articles belonging to
the murdered woman.

The contents of the trunk offer an interesting
footnote to Western history, the more valued possessions of a "lady of the line" in the 1860's. In
addition to the diamond pin, the sable cape, muff,
and wristlets, and the silk and velvet opera hood

already mentioned, Millain had stolen one pair of large, coral ear drops; a jet set consisting of a cross, breastpin, and ear drops; a long, gold guard chain with miniature scissors, thimble, and needle case, all of gold, attached as charms; one set of enameled sleeve buttons; a silver brick with the name "Julia" engraved upon it; a heavy gold ring with the initials "J.J. to N.M." engraved inside, and outside "R.S.M."; three miniature pillars, Masonic emblems, set in gold and silver standards; one pair of red silk stockings; a rich cape, a black silk dress, a plaid silk dress, a scarlet silk dress, a purple silk dress, and a silk breakfast cape trimmed with swan's-down; a silver cup containing the initials "J.C.B."; a gold watch; silk handkerchiefs with Julia's name; and silk cords and various pieces of gilded lace.

Numerous witnesses came forward at the trial of Millain, which began on June 26, 1867, to identify the items found in Millain's trunk and other items, including watches, dresses, and jewelry, which he had stolen from Julia Bulette and either pawned or sold to individuals. Among the witnesses was Hank Monk, the famous stage driver of the Sierra, who identified a watch which he had first given to Annie Smith in Carson, who had, in turn, given it to Julia to have repaired in Virginia City. Monk testified that he had "seen Julia Bulette on at least two occasions." Otherwise undescribed, the number of the watch was given as 3,375. All of the valuables were ultimately sold at auction by Nye, the jeweler, acting for the County.

Millain had informally admitted the murder to the police shortly after he was arrested. But at his trial he pleaded not guilty to the charge, although admitting that he had participated in the robbery. He claimed that two men, Douglas and Dillon, had actually committed the crime while he had remained outside Julia's house, and that he had no knowledge that murder was to be done until he heard the men talking of it afterward. Again, he accused a man named Blair of the murder—seemingly an accusation made at random, for when Blair and Millain were placed in the same room, Millain failed to recognize him. The jury, however, in spite of an able defense by Millain's lawyer, believed Millain to be guilty. Since they did so, their feelings and the feelings of the Comstock citizenry are perhaps best reflected in the summation of the prosecution, presented by District Attorney Bishop:

"Although this community has, in times past, seen blood run like water, yet in most cases there was some cause brought forward in justification of the deed, some pretext. But on the morning of the 20th of January last, this community, so hardened by previous deeds of blood, was struck dumb with horror by a deed which carried dread to the heart of every one—a deed more fiendish, more horrible than ever before perpetrated on this side of the snowy Sierra. Julia Bulette was found lying dead in her bed, foully murdered, and stiff and cold in her clotted gore. True, she was a woman of easy virtue. Yet hundreds in this city have had cause to bless her name for her many acts of kindness and charity. So much worse the crime. That woman probably had more real, warm friends in this community than any other; yet there was found at last a human being so fiendish and base as to crawl to her bedside in the dead hour of the night, and with violent hands, beat and strangle her to death—not for revenge, but in order to plunder her of these very articles of clothing and jewelry we see before us. What inhuman, unparalled barbarity!"

Nevertheless, Millain's lawyer, Charles E. DeLong, appealed the case to the Supreme Court of Nevada, sitting at Carson. A rehearing, however, was refused, and on February 22, 1868, the case was returned to the First District Court in Virginia City, where Millain was sentenced, on February 27, to be hanged on the twenty-fourth day of April between ten in the morning and four o'clock in the afternoon.

During his confinement in jail, Millain was lionized by the good ladies of the Comstock who brought pâté de foie gras, jellies, wines, and other delicacies to him. Some refused to believe his guilt, while others felt that to rid the community of Julia was not a crime to be punished by death. They went so far as to circulate a petition for the commutation of the sentence to life imprisonment, but *The Territorial Enterprise* scotched its success with the blunt statement: "We believe that the man will be hung. If he is not, we do not know where a fit subject for hanging is to be found."

Work on the gallows was commenced April 19, 1868, and they were placed on display at Benham's carpenter shop on Taylor Street between B and C Streets on April 22. From July, 1867, to the time of the execution, also, picture postcards of Millain had been placed on sale at Johnny Croall's Virginia News Depot, opposite Wells, Fargo and Company's office on C Street. News of the murder and of the expected hanging had reached all parts of the state, so that on April 24 the city was crowded with visitors, and the scenes in town and at the site of the execution were those of a Western holiday.

According to the press of the day, the whole of B Street was a living, swaying mass of human beings. At eleven-thirty in the morning, a heavily curtained carriage was driven to the front of the courthouse, where Millain was imprisoned on the ground floor. The carriage was at once surrounded by forty special deputy sheriffs armed with Henry rifles. Shortly thereafter, the National Guard, numbering about sixty men, marched in full uniform from their armory and formed a second square outside the deputy sheriffs. A lane of bayonets was also formed from the door of the courthouse to the waiting carriage and, as the crowd pressed and pushed forward, the order was given to load with ball cartridges. Then Millain, accompanied by Father Manogue of Virginia City and Father Clarke of Carson, stepped quickly from the building into the carriage—so rapidly, in fact, that the morbid crowd had barely a glimpse of the prisoner whom they could no longer see in the curtained carriage.

While the regular police cleared the line of march, the deputies and men of the National Guard formed a double line on either side of the carriage. This was followed by two other carriages, one carrying the physicians, and the other the representatives of the press. A carriage with a black-draped coffin brought up the rear.

The route to the place of execution, a natural amphitheater one mile to the north of the city, was lined with the curious, while in advance of the procession, men, women, and children, Mexicans, Paiutes, and Chinese swarmed to the northward. The gallows had been erected a short distance above the Jewish Cemetery and about a hundred and fifty yards below the Geiger Grade. Leaving the carriage on the Grade, the prisoner was marched to the scaffold, where he heard the death warrant read by Sheriff Leconey. Although Millain had a somewhat haggard look due to his long prison confinement, his manner was calm and his demeanor firm. He read a prepared statement in French, his native tongue, spoke extemporaneously for two or three minutes in French and then, in very good English, thanked the ladies of Virginia City for their interest in him and concern for his welfare while he was in prison. He knelt while both priests prayed for him, kissed them both, and, as the noose was being adjusted, continued to pray himself.

The black cap was pulled down over his face and the instant that its strings were pulled taut, the trap was released and Millain passed to eternity.

Millain was buried in the Catholic Cemetery, two miles north of the town, but the location of his grave has been lost. Julia's grave, however, on Flowery Hill, has been carefully tended, its white picket fence repainted from time to time. All other graves in the cemetery are neglected; weather-beaten picket fences lean awry, and headstones have crumbled. Alone, respected and honored by Virginia City, the grave of Julia Bulette, a "lady of the line," marks the cemetery.

TO DIE WITH BOOTS ON

Approximately twenty thousand men died violently on the Western frontier between 1830 and the turn of the present century, from the time of the trapper to the advent of law and order. Included in this estimate, of course, are all men—Indians, Chinese, Mexicans, Americans—who met each other in conflict outside of the law and outside of legal warfare. It is probable, even, that this figure is low, since records frequently were not kept, were inaccurate, or have been destroyed.

In the southeastern corner of New Mexico alone, between 1875 and 1881, more than two hundred men were killed in cattle wars, rustling, and general lawlessness. Four hundred men are listed as dying violent deaths in Nevada between 1860 and 1880. Henry Plummer's infamous gang in Idaho and Montana reputedly accounted for the death of some two hundred men, and the sheep wars of Colorado and Wyoming added to the toll. Individual killers with three and four deaths to their credit were common throughout the whole area, and sheriffs and desperadoes like Billy the Kid, the vicious and brutal Sam Brown, Wyatt Earp, Clay Allison, John Slaughter, Tom Horn, and Boone Helm had many more. Single killings were of such frequent occurrence that they received only passing attention, and the phrase "a man for breakfast" was a standard and accepted joke throughout the whole region.

A great percentage of the killings were, according to the code of the time, justified. There was no law and order to begin with, and even when so-called law finally arrived, it was often in the dubious form of sheriffs whose integrity was frequently open to question. For defense of life and property, men relied on themselves and their companions. The six-shooter, the Sharps and Henry rifles, the Spencer carbine, the Winchester and the Remington ruled. The honest man employed them only in case of necessity and in self-defense. The lawless used them for robbery and murder. But even among the lawless, those who prided their reputations never shot to kill without giving their opponents a fair chance. To kill an unarmed man, to shoot from behind or to shoot from ambush, was vicious murder and not condoned by the code of the West. Such murders—as distinct from open killings—were an admission of cowardice, and the coward was not welcomed. It was more frequently he than the gunfighter who decorated the end of a rope. Whatever he might boastfully think of himself, he was despised for a nerveless weakling, and his death was good riddance.

But both the coward and the outlaw, the bogus article and the real, helped to populate the hundreds of Boothills in the West. The lead of Missouri made no distinctions. The graves of the men are unmarked in most instances, overgrown with sagebrush and cedar, and the wooden headstones have crumbled to dust. In Virginia City, where some hundred men died with their boots on, at best the graves of only one or two may still be located. As well-cared-for as the graves are at Tombstone, there are many unknowns. And throughout the West, the traveler will still find, off the beaten track of the main roads, isolated graves marked only with a few stones—either six-by-three depressions in the ground where the loose earth has settled, or slightly raised and unmistakable mounds. Whose they are no one knows, and to the violent events of the day there are no witnesses.

With identification of the graves lost, the men themselves, nevertheless, remain legends, remembered in the towns where they gained their brief fame, or more widely known when their deeds were bruited from one end of the frontier to the other. There can be no question that they "went under" and "passed in their checks" with a dramatic flair unequaled elsewhere.

There was Pat Garrett saying, "I was just a shade too quick for him." There was Wyatt Earp advising Cockeyed Frank Loving, "Take your time and make your shots count," and Frank slowly shooting into the body of Levi Richardson while Richardson theatrically fanned his gun and his wild shots missed. It was Kit Carson "obliging" a boasting bully with a pistol shot that shattered his hand and arm. It was Johnny Ringo asking Frank Leslie a damned impertinent question, "Did you ever shoot anybody in front?" And Johnny Ringo resting under a tree with a bullet in his head, and nobody asking Leslie any questions. It was Ike Stockton killed at Durango, and Bert Noble shot in Trinidad. It was Kelly riding up to Bob Ford's saloon in Creede and saying, "Hello, Bob" over the barrel of a gun. It was Buckshot Roberts, crippled and

wounded almost to death, standing off thirteen
fighting men led by Dick Brewer and Billy the Kid.
It was Billy the Kid shooting Bob Ollinger from
the balcony of the Lincoln jail, breaking the gun
and throwing it down on his hated enemy, "Take
that to hell with you!" And Arnett, in Montana,
shot at a game of cards and dying, with a death
grip on a six-shooter in one hand and a hand of
cards in the other—and buried that way.

There was Clay Allison finding the boastful
Chunk Colbert in a restaurant in Cimarron and
calling the bluff with an order for "Coffee and
pistols for two." They sat facing each other, stirring
the coffee with their guns, knowing that one, perhaps two, would never rise from the table. Chunk
broke first and fired wild, and before he could pull
the trigger again Clay Allison had kicked the table
hard against his enemy and killed him with a single
shot over the left eye.

There was Clay Allison again, with Mason Bowman, each with a bottle, drunk, dancing around
and around on a dusty road, Allison trying to draw
his gun faster than Bowman. He tried again at
Henry Lambert's hotel, the St. James in Cimarron,
where twenty-six men had been shot. The two had
the whole bar to themselves and Lambert, who
served up the whisky, bobbed and ducked all afternoon—"more than a hundred times"—but Allison
never drew faster than Bowman. When men went

for their guns, there was usually shooting, but this once there was none. Bowman did not want to kill Allison. And Allison, who had driven Bat Masterson to cover in Dodge City, knew that he had met his gun match and that if he were to fire at Bowman, he himself would also be dead.

Just as Clay Allison had warned Chunk, so also did the bad men who aspired to any reputation as "chief." Eldorado Johnny had such aspirations on the Comstock and went gunning for Langford Peel, commonly known as Farmer Peel. Peel was a tough fighter and fearless, and Eldorado Johnny knew that he might wind up with a grave rather than a reputation, so he proceeded to ready himself for either outcome of the fight. He went first to the barber shop, where he got a shave and had his hair curled and his boots highly polished. Then, dressing in his best outfit, he proceeded to the saloon where Peel was drinking and called him out into the street. Peel accepted the challenge and came out shooting, killing Eldorado Johnny with three well-placed bullets. Johnny made as elegant-looking a corpse as it had ever been the roughs' honor to bury. They carried him to the cemetery with considerable pomp, and as the cortege wound back to C Street the band gaily played "When Johnny Comes Marching Home Again."

Peel himself went to his death in Helena, Montana, in 1867. In a quarrel with a man named Bull,

he started for his gun, when Bull cried out that he
was not armed. "Go and arm yourself, then, and
when you come back, come fighting." Bull obtained
a gun and returned to the saloon just as Peel was
coming out the door. Bull fired three shots, and Peel
fell dead before he had had a chance to draw his
gun.

Similarly, at Austin, Nevada, in August, 1868, a
man named Vance, who claimed to be a bad man
from Montana, provoked a fight with Irish Tom
Carberry which for sheer drama validates the motion picture and the romanticized "western." Vance
told Irish Tom that he was going to kill him. Carberry was unarmed at the time and told Vance so,
at which Vance said, "Go and heel yourself and
come back shooting." Carberry, his back to Vance,
quietly left the saloon and walked down the street
to obtain a pistol. When he had armed himself with
a six-shooter, he carelessly sauntered back along
the now-deserted street. Vance, who was on the
lookout, immediately began to fire. Carberry, gun
held in hand at his side, walked unhesitatingly
forward into close range in spite of the repeated
shots of his enemy.

When he had reached a position which suited
him—and not until then—Carberry rested his
pistol across his arm, took careful aim, and shot
Vance dead.

Like Peel, Vance, Carberry, and Allison, the best

of them gave each other a fighting chance. Wyatt Earp never went for his gun until his enemy had gone for his. Billy Breakenridge, during the forty years he served as peace officer and sheriff, never shot at a man until he had already been shot at. A sheepherder and a cowboy fired at each other in Colorado until the cowboy shouted, "Don't shoot, I'm empty." To which the sheepherder replied, "Well, then, load up while I wait." Curly Bill gave Jim Wallace ample warning in Gayleyville when he called him a "Lincoln County son-of-a-bitch" before going for his guns. The men in the Lincoln County war, in the Harold War—on the Pecos and Ruidoso—and those involved in the Graham-Tewksbury feud were fully warned and, by and large, gave each other the even break of the West.

Where the killers did not abide by the code, they were branded murderers and were given short shrift in death. When Billy Morton, Tom Hill, Jesse Evans, Frank Baker, and others rode as a posse toward the ranch of the English cattle rancher, Tunstall, to serve an attachment, they met Tunstall himself, in company with Billy the Kid, Dick Brewer, and John Middleton. Tunstall happened to be alone at the moment, the others still some distance away on the hills. Tunstall dismounted from his horse and walked toward the men of the posse, saying, "You wouldn't hurt me, boys, would you?" Tom Hill, who had previously threatened to kill

Tunstall, ordered him to throw up his hands. Then Hill deliberately shot him dead. Billy the Kid vowed vengeance on the men of the posse, and when, at a later meeting, he had Baker and Morton defenseless before him, he shot them both mercilessly while they were on their knees begging for life. They had not given the even break. They did not deserve it themselves.

Sam Brown, like Tom Hill, was also a coward who played the role of bad man all too effectively. He was of medium height, stocky, with a florid complexion, and coarse red hair and whiskers. He swaggered through the streets and barrooms of Virginia City, Nevada, heavy-voiced and insolent to those who were unarmed, wearing a large revolver and huge bowie knife slung to a belt about his waist. He was simply a brutal monster, with every instinct brutish, utterly mean, treacherous, and an arrant coward. He killed only when his courage had been inflamed by drink; and then, deliberately and cold-bloodedly, without excuse or provocation, murdered his victim only when he knew perfectly well that he himself was in no danger. He never once dared to provoke a quarrel with anyone equally well-armed, nor did he, after engaging in a quarrel, ever invite an opponent out to a fair field of battle. That he was not sooner killed himself is simply an indication of the lawlessness of the Com stock in 1861.

During his lifetime, Brown killed an estimated thirteen men in the West. His most revolting crime took place in a barroom on C Street in 1861, the same year in which he himself was to die. A young and inoffensive miner, known only as McKenzie, accidentally brushed the "bad man's" elbow at the bar. Brown turned, glowering at his victim, whom he recognized as friendless and unknown in the camp. He seized the terrified youth by the throat and—"Brown ran a knife into his victim, and then turned it around, completely cutting the heart out, then wiped his bloody knife and lay down on a billiard table and went to sleep."

The bully picked at last on the wrong man, a peaceful farmer and inn keeper, Vansickle, whose place was two miles beyond Genoa. On July 6, 1861, his birthday, Brown boasted that he would "have a man for supper" and selected Vansickle as his victim. When Brown rode up on horseback, however, Vansickle had just time enough to run into the house and seize a shotgun. Brown, dismayed at resistance, rode off, but Vansickle determined to end the ruffian's life and not be subject to further attacks. Mounting his own horse, he rode in pursuit and overtook Brown at dusk, just as the latter was dismounting. "Upon seeing his pursuer, mortal terror seized upon the ruffian; abject, unutterable fear sealed his lips; a spasmodic, agonizing yell of despair forced itself from his mouth . . ." Vansickle

discharged both barrels into his breast, and Brown
was dead. An inquest was held the following day
and the Western verdict was that Vansickle "had
shown good sense, and, instead of deserving pun-
ishment, he should be rewarded for having thus
rid the community of this brutal and cowardly villain."

There were cowards like John Clark, a member
of the Opdyke gang in Boise City. Clark disliked
Reuben Raymond, who had testified against him
at a trial for horse stealing, and cornered Raymond
when the latter was unarmed. Raymond bared his
chest, saying, "I am entirely unarmed, but if you
wish to shoot me down like a dog, there is nothing
to hinder you. Give me a chance, and I will fight
you in any way you choose, though I have nothing
against you." Clark gave him no chance, but took
deliberate aim and murdered his victim. Clark was
summarily hanged within a few minutes by irate
citizens.

Individual lawlessness and that of the organized
gangs, such as the Opdyke and Plummer, in Idaho
and Montana, and the Coon Hole Gang, in Utah,
brought about the early establishment of the vigilantes, particularly in the towns and camps of the
mining country. The vigilantes were not in any
sense lynch mobs nor can they be compared with
them, since the gangs themselves were lawless,
whereas the vigilante organizations were the fore-

runners of established law and order. They operated under a code of Western fairness, trying the outlaws according to all the evidence in hand and resorting to the death penalty only when repeated warnings and all other efforts to control them had failed. As long as the outlaws killed off each other, the citizens overlooked their actions and allowed the dog-eat-dog shootings to continue. But when the desperadoes flagrantly robbed the innocent, jumped claims, held up the mails, committed murder and other crimes terrorizing a whole region, the vigilantes acted. There came into being the famous signatures posted throughout the territory which struck terror to the heart of the guilty—the XXX of Idaho, the 601 of Nevada, and the 3-7-77 of Montana.

The gunfighters of the West feared, above everything else, the rope, and, when any choice was offered, preferred fighting it out to the death with guns rather than risk hanging. This was particularly true in the cattle country and among cowboys. In the mining camps, where the deeds of a gang were known, the vigilantes acted swiftly and as a body, permitting no resistance. The desperadoes were seized quietly, quickly tried, and hanged. The outlaws, in many cases, were so certain of their strength as a gang that they refused to believe they could be hanged, and for this reason frequently offered no resistance to "arrest." The vigilantes, however, clearly demonstrated that they meant business, and law came to the land.

The most infamous of the gangs in the West was Henry Plummer's, which operated out of the towns of Bannack, Virginia City, and Nevada in Montana. Plummer, who was neat-appearing, seemingly honest, suave, and well-educated in terms of the frontier, had managed to have himself appointed sheriff of Virginia City and the surrounding region. And as sheriff he was naturally in a key position to organize depredations and to direct the activity of outlaws under his command. For a considerable time he was not suspected, and his men operated with impunity, until at last the weary citizens took matters into their own hands and in January, 1864, put an end to Plummer and his men.

The manner in which the outlaws met their death, their approach to the scaffold, was often indicative of their cowardly natures. Men who had brutally murdered and who themselves had callously taken life, showing no pity or mercy, groveled in the face of what they knew to be the unalterable vigilante verdict. Some few, on the other hand, faced death with great bravery. Andrew J. Huff, who was hanged by the people of Surprise Valley, Nevada, in 1868, saw that there was no escape from the verdict and took the matter of hanging philosophically. With his hands untied, he climbed upon a fence underneath the temporary gallows, adjusted the rope around his own neck, and jumped off, thus literally becoming his own hangman. And one brave member of the Plummer gang, hanged in Montana, was taken to a near-by barn where a rope had been thrown over the cross-beam. In lieu of any prepared trap or drop, he was told to mount a ladder. With the rope around his neck, he turned to the men below: "Gentlemen, I am not used to this business, never having been hung before. Shall I jump off or slide off?" Upon being told to jump, he said, "All right, goodbye," and leaped into the air as calmly as though he were going swimming. Other men, knowing the moment the trap was to be released, jumped into the air of their own accord in order to be assured of a good drop. Bill Bunton, who was hanged by the Montana vigilantes at the gate of Louis Demarest's corral in January, 1864, was asked if he had any last request. "No, all I want is a mountain three hundred feet high to jump off. I shall give the time myself . . . one, two, three . . . here goes!"

But when five members of the Plummer gang—Boone Helm, Hayes Lyon, Jack Gallagher or Gallaher, Frank Parish, and Clubfoot George Lane—were hanged together on January 14, 1864, there were violent and difficult scenes. Gallaher was a coward throughout, and spent his last moments cursing the vigilantes and pitying himself. At one point he drew a pocketknife, threatening to stab himself. A vigilante told him to put it down or he would blow his head off. Gallaher complied. He tried once to make merry in a ghastly fashion. "How do I look, boys, with a halter around my neck?" Gallaher also continually asked for whisky, which was freely given him. At the very last, when the rope was tight around his neck, he asked for "just one more drink" which the vigilantes supplied. He drank then a whole tumblerful, leaning forward against the rope. Boone Helm, as depraved a villain as ever set foot on the Western stage, scorned Gallaher's weakness. Among his many crimes, Helm had once killed a companion in the mountains in winter and eaten his flesh. When asked about it, he had replied, "Of course I did. You don't think I was damned fool enough to starve to death." Helm had no pity for anyone else and none for himself. "I have looked at death in all forms and I am not afraid to die." As George Lane swung from the gallows, Helm's comment was, "There's one gone to hell." As Gallaher died, he callously exclaimed, "Kick away, old fellow. My turn next. I'll be in hell with you in a minute!"

Plummer, the leader of the gang and the man fully responsible for all the crimes in the region, was hanged with Ned Ray and Buck Stinson. Ray and Stinson died hard, cursing and fighting. Ray, who had been loosely pinioned, got one hand loose and his fingers between the noose and his neck. Plummer himself was frantic at the prospect of death. He offered to leave the country forever, he asked to be chained down for life in a cabin, wanted a jury trial, asked to see his sister-in-law, declared he was too wicked to die, implored time to settle his affairs, and cried and begged for his life. He even asked the vigilantes to cut off his ears, hands, and tongue rather than hang him. Then he wanted to say his prayers, by which time the vigilantes had had enough, and ordered him to say them from the gallows. At the last he requested a good drop, and vigilantes raised him by hand as high as possible. Dutch John Wagner, like Plummer, also asked the vigilantes to cut off his legs and arms rather than kill him, but at the last reconciled himself. "How long will it take to die? I have never seen anyone hanged." When he was informed that it would be brief, he seemed pleased.

Steve Marshland asked to be pardoned because of his youth, to which the vigilantes replied that if he was old enough to kill, he was old enough to die. Cy Skinner broke and ran, asking his captors to shoot, but they refused his request. Joseph Slade crept about on his hands and knees. "My God! My God! Must I die? Oh, my poor wife, my poor wife! My God, men, you can't mean that I'm to die!"

John Stewart, who was hanged at Aurora, Nevada, requested only that he be allowed all the whisky he wanted from the time of leaving his cell to the moment of hanging. This was freely granted and a bottle holder stood by his side throughout. Sufficiently inspired at the last, he delivered himself of the following Western soliloquy: "If you take the mountain road, you will be murdered by Indians; if you take the trail, you will find no water and die of thirst. I must take the trail, and in fifteen minutes will be choked to death." In the same town, the dreaded Citizens Safety Committee seized four desperadoes who had been guilty of many brutal murders in the region—John Dailey, Three Fingered Jack, James Masterson, and John McDowell. Governor Nye, attempting to maintain complete order in the Territory, wired Samuel Youngs, one of the County Commissioners: "There must be no disturbances." Young laconically wired back: "Peace and order prevail. Four men will be hanged in half an hour."

Gunfighters for whom the West still has a certain admiration, determined and fearless sheriffs, outlaws, and cowardly murderers for whom there can be no sympathy—the great majority died with their boots on. When officers of the law died so, it was considered an honor, a death in the performance of duty. When the outlaws fell with their boots on, they often asked to have them removed, for they superstitiously felt—according to the custom and belief of the West—that they had died with guilt evident. Not naturally and peacefully in bed, but fighting and dying before their time in the streets and on the range. When Billy Clanton was killed by the Earps in the O.K. Corral fight, his last words were, "Pull off my boots. I promised my mother I'd never die with my boots on." When Tom Peasley and Martin Barnhardt suddenly shot it out at the Ormsby House in Carson City, each killing the other, Peasley's friends gathered around him. "Is Barnhardt dead?" he whispered. "He is," they replied. " 'Tis well. Pull my boots off, and send for my brother Andy . . ."

PARSON RALPH RILEY, a Bostonian and
a Presbyterian, preached many sermons in the
West of the '60's and '70's, attended many more,
and always kept an observant eye cocked to the
mores of the land. He reported with good humor a
church service which he attended, held under a
spreading oak by the Truckee River on the eastern
slope of the Sierra Nevada, a service which ended
in an uproarious row.

"You talk of your church rows here in the East, why, they are no more like what we used to have out there than a hurdy-gurdy and monkey show is like a Barnum circus. Out yonder they were grand with the grandeur of the Rocky Mountains and Sierras. We had none of your little quarrels you have hereabouts with small Christians in them saying mean things against each other in the dark. No, when a sister in Nevada buckled on the armor to do battle against the Midianites she was a Deborah, when a brother drew his sword he was a Gideon . . . .

"I witnessed a church row on a grand scale once in Nevada. The congregation was made up of silver miners, gamblers, lumbermen, and gold hunters. Some of them were Welshmen with their wives, with a dozen or so Indians standing on the outer edge of the congregation.

"When the preacher got through his sermon, he asked them to name the place of the next meeting. Pine Nob Morgan suggested that we meet at Sister Ferguson's place in Roaring Canyon. Mrs. Morgan jumped up and said: 'Not if I know it, by gosh!' Pine Nob told her to shut her mouth or he would put a spur of the Sierras in it. California Jack from Cedar Gulch told Pine Nob that he was no gentleman, and didn't know how to behave himself in church. Mrs. Brown screamed that Pine Nob was seen going too often up to Roaring Canyon. Andy

Jackson asked her what sort of a boarding house she kept when Brown was in the mountains? One of the boarders got up and said he would make mincemeat of Andy and feed him to the dogs. Jemima Ferguson asked where was last Sunday's collection? 'It was drunk at the Red Gulch Saloon!' shouted a half dozen angry voices. The preacher raised his arms to pronounce the benediction, but they must have supposed that he was waving them on to deeds of valor, for every man and woman of them sprung to their feet and at each other like fury. Then you would see their eyes glare like Carnegie's furnaces, their fists rising into the upper air like a peak of the Rockies, and the sound of their screaming and shouting was like the roaring of the Atlantic when a sou'wester is blowing. Red Dog, one of the Indians present, gave a war whoop and leaped up from the ground four feet, and then ran around yelping, as he used to when after scalps.

"I like first-class church rows with first-class Christians in them. Then the air smells like the atmosphere of Nevada and the music enters your soul like 'Scots wha hae wi' Wallace bled.'"

And when the same Parson Riley, a newcomer to the ways of a mining camp, was asked to preach a funeral service over a gambler, he confused the identity of the corpse with that of a "sinner" in the congregation. Riley denounced gambling as a curse, and the supposed dead man as one of the

worst specimens of the gambling fraternity. Had
his sermon been gentle, the "sinner" might have
had no objections to hearing his own funeral, but
as it was his wrath boiled over. Leaping to his feet
and pointing his revolver at Riley, he shouted:
"Don't shake me over hell that way, pard! Don't
you do it, or I will blow your cabbage head into the
next century!" Meeting Riley on the street the next
day, he apologized for his rudeness at the service:
"I am glad now that I did not kill you; but take
my advice, young man, and never preach a funeral
sermon like that one again. You fellows of the cloth
imagine that all of our profession are going to the
devil when we die, but perhaps we will stand as
good a show as yourselves. At any rate, be wise
as a serpent and harmless as a dove when you
preach our funeral sermons in Nevada."

There is the story also of a visitor wandering
down the deserted streets of Goldfield, after that
town had "busted." The 200-room hotel housed
three customers. Homes were empty, stores closed
and shuttered, and saloons vacant. Progressing
along the street, the visitor came to the Episcopal
Church, its doors also shut. But hanging on the front
of the edifice was an intimate, informative, and
forthright sign: CHURCH CLOSED. JESUS GONE TO
TONOPAH.

Again, during the winter and summer of 1885,
little or no rain had fallen in Arizona. The land

was unusually dry, and the cattlemen, contriving
means to save their herds, held a meeting at Willcox, which Big Dan Ming was asked to open with
a prayer. Ming, whose cow ranch was in the Ara-
vaipa Canyon in Graham County, rose to his feet,
nothing daunted by the task:

"Oh, Lord, I'm about to round you up for a good
plain talk. Now, Lord, I ain't like these fellows who
come bothering you every day. This is the first time
I ever tackled you for anything and if you will
only grant this, I'll promise never to bother you
again. We want rain, good Lord, and we want it
bad, and we ask you to send us some. But if you
can't or don't want to send us any, for Christ's sake
don't make it rain up around Hooker's or Leitch's
ranges, but treat us all alike. Amen."

The stories illustrate not untruthfully something
of the Westerner's direct approach to his God. There
is no namby-pamby groveling or fear in his relationship to his Maker. Nor is there any dry, thin-
lipped moralistic code forcing the Westerner to ex-
clude certain members of the community from
relationship with God. When sermons were delivered out-of-doors or in saloons, where was the
righteous hypocrite to point the finger of scorn?
Were not all men beings, the hurdy-gurdy girl and
the gambler, the outlaw and the drinker?

Nowhere in the annals of the West is this "live
and let live" philosophy more clearly shown than

in the classical funeral oration delivered by W. H. Knickerbocker over the body of Riley Grannan at the boom camp of Rawhide, Nevada, on April 3, 1908. Knickerbocker was a miner who had once been a preacher; Grannan had been a gambler.

Well-educated, trained for the ministry, Knickerbocker first served as minister in a fashionable church in New Orleans and later at Trinity Church in Los Angeles. Independent in thought and original in ideas, however, his utterances ran counter to those of the Church authorities. He was tried for heresy—in Southern California be it noted—but acquitted. The experience, however, embittered him and he resigned his pastorate and withdrew from the clergy. He came to Nevada and, following the booms, drifted first to Tonopah, then to Goldfield, and finally to Rawhide, where he worked in the mines and where he met Grannan.

Riley Grannan was one of the nation's big-time gamblers and plungers, and had come to the new and explosive camp of Rawhide with a roll of twenty thousand dollars staked him by friends in Reno. Grannan opened a gambling house but lost his stake. Then won, only to lose again. Knickerbocker and Grannan became friends in the wild town, the ex-preacher drawn to the gambler, admiring the equanimity with which the latter accepted both the winning and losing cards of fate.

One night, however, after deep losses at the gaming table, Grannan toured the saloons and bright spots of Stingaree Gulch, drinking heavily and exposing himself needlessly to the raw March weather. He contracted pneumonia and died shortly thereafter, on April 1.

On April 3rd, Knickerbocker left his work on a windlass to speak the farewell words over the body of his friend.

Grannan's body, lying in a rude coffin built by some miner, had been carried by wagon to a little cubby hole of a vaudeville theater in the back of a Rawhide saloon. The surroundings were bare. And the audience was one of the toughest in the West of its day—gamblers, floaters and adventurers, dance-hall girls and gaudily dressed women of the district, miners and prospectors. Knickerbocker, wearing boots and rough mining clothes, stood by the coffin, resting one hand upon the unfinished boards. There was nothing incongruous about the scene to the participants. This was Rawhide.

The sermon contained bitter and gentle words, and words that brought tears to the eyes of the hardened crowd. True, it contained the florid passages of the oratorical South, yet, as purple passages go, Knickerbocker's are extraordinary and deserve preservation on antiquarian grounds alone. But the core of the oration is in its realism, Western realism, determined by the character of Grannan and the audience which Knickerbocker addressed, determined by Knickerbocker's own wrecked life and the camp of Rawhide.

Knickerbocker began simply, and the miners, gamblers, and women of the town listened:

"I feel that it is incumbent upon me to state that in standing here I occupy no ministerial or prelatic position. I am simply a prospector. I make no claims whatever to moral merit or to religion except the religion of humanity, the brotherhood of man. I stand among you today simply as a man among men, feeling that I can shake hands and say 'brother' to the vilest man or woman that ever lived. If there should come to you anything of moral admonition through what I may say, it comes not from any sense of moral superiority, but from the depth of my experience.

"Riley Grannan was born in Paris, Kentucky, about forty years ago. I suppose he dreamed all the dreams of boyhood. They blossomed into phenomenal success along financial lines at times during his life. I am told that from the position of a bell boy in a hotel he rose rapidly to be a celebrity of world-wide fame. He was one of the greatest plungers, probably, that the continent has ever produced.

"He died the day before yesterday in Rawhide.

"This is a very brief statement. You have the birth and the period of the grave. Who can fill the interim? Who can speak of his hopes and fears?

Who can solve the mystery of his quiet hours that only himself knew? I cannot.

"He was born in the Sunny Southland—in Kentucky. He died in Rawhide.

"Here is the beginning and the end. I wonder if we can see in this a picture of what Ingersoll said at the grave of his brother—'Whether it be near the shore or in mid ocean or among the breakers, at the last a wreck must mar the end of one and all.'

"He was born in the Sunny Southland, where brooks and rivers run musically through the luxuriant soil; where the magnolia grandiflora like white stars grow in a firmament of green; where crystal lakes dot the greensward and the softest summer breezes dimple the wave-lips into kisses for the lilies on the shore; where the air is resonant with the warbled melody of a thousand sweet-voiced birds and redolent of the perfume of many flowers. This was the beginning. He died in Rawhide, where in winter the shoulders of the mountains are wrapped in garments of ice and in summer the blistering rays of the sun beat down upon the skeleton ribs of the desert. Is this a picture of universal human life?

"Sometimes when I look over the circumstances of human life, a curse rises to my lips, and, if you will allow me, I will say here that I speak from an individual point of view. I cannot express other than my own views. If I run counter to yours, at least give me credit for a desire to be honest.

"When I see the ambitions of man defeated; when I see him struggling with mind and body in the only legitimate prayer he can make to accomplish some end; when I see his aim and purpose frustrated by a fortuitous combination of circumstances over which he has no control; when I see the outstretched hand, just about to grasp the flag of victory, take instead the emblem of defeat, I ask: What is life? Dreams, awakening and death.

"Not so with Riley Grannan. If I have gauged his character correctly, he accepted the circumstances surrounding his as the mystic officials to whom the universe had delegated its whole office concerning him. He seemed to accept both defeat and victory with equanimity. He was a man whose exterior was as placid and gentle as I have ever seen, and yet when we look back over his meteoric past we can readily understand, if this statement be true, that he was absolutely invincible in spirit. If you will allow me, I will use a phrase most of you are acquainted with. He was a 'dead game sport.' I say it not irreverently, but fill the phrase as full of practical human philosophy as it will hold, and I believe that when you say one is a 'dead game sport' you have reached the climax of human philosophy.

"I know that there are those who will condemn

him. There are those who believe today that he is
reaping the reward of a misspent life. There are
those who are dominated by medieval creeds. To
those I have no words to say in regard to him. They
are ruled by the skeleton hand of the past and fail
to see the moral beauty of a character lived outside
their puritanical ideas. His goodness was not of
that type, but of the type that finds expression in
a word of cheer to a discouraged brother; the type
that finds expression in quiet deeds of charity; the
type that finds expression in friendship, the sweet-
est flower that blooms along the dusty highway of
life; the type that finds expression in manhood.

"He lived in the world of sport. I do not mince
my words. I am telling what I believe to be true.
In the world of sport—hilarity sometimes, and
maybe worse—he left the impress of his character
on this world, and through the medium of his financial power he was able with his money to
brighten the lives of its inhabitants. He wasted it
so the world says. But did it ever occur to you that
the most sinful men and women who live in this
world are still men and women? Did it ever occur
to you that the men and women who inhabit the
night-world are still men and women? A little happiness brought into their lives means as much to
them as happiness brought into the lives of the
straight and the good. If you can take one ray of
sunlight into their night-life and thereby bring

them one single hour of happiness, I believe you are a benefactor.

"Riley Grannan may have 'wasted' some of his money this way.

"Did you ever stop and think how God does not put all his sunbeams into corn, potatoes, and flour? Did you ever notice the prodigality with which He scatters these sunbeams over the universe? Contemplate:

"God flings the auroral beauties 'round the cold shoulders of the north; hangs the quivering picture of the mirage above the palpitating heart of the desert; scatters the sunbeams like lamellated gold upon the bosoms of myriad lakes that gem the verdant robe of nature; spangles the canopy of night with star-jewels, and silvers the world with the reflected beams from Cynthia's mellow face; hangs the gorgeous crimson curtain of the occident across the sleeping-room of the sun; wakes the coy maid of dawn to step timidly from her boudoir to climb the steps of the orient and fling wide-open the gates of the morning. Then, tripping o'er the landscape, kissing the flowers in her flight, she wakes the birds to herald with their music the coming of her King, who floods the world with refulgent gold. Wasted sunbeams, these? I say to you that the man who by the use of his money or power is able to smooth one wrinkle from the brow of care, is able to change one moan or sob into a song, is able to wipe away one tear and in its place put a jewel of joy—this man is a public benefactor.

"I believe that some of Riley Grannan's money was 'wasted' in this way.

"We stand at last in the presence of the Great Mystery. I know nothing about it, nor do you. We may have our hopes, but no knowledge. I do not know whether there be a future life or not; I do not say there is not. I simply say I do not know. I have watched the wicket gate closed behind many and many a pilgrim. No word has come back to me. The gate is closed. Across the chasm is the gloomy cloud of death. I say I do not know. And, if you will allow this expression, I do not know whether it is best that my dust or his at last should go to feed the roots of the grasses, the sagebrush or the flowers, to be blown in protean forms by the law of persistency of force, or whether it is best that I continue in personal identity beyond what we call death. If this be all, 'after life's fever, he sleeps well; . . . . Nothing can harm him further.' God knows what is best.

"This may be infidelity, but if it is, I would like to know what faith means. I came into this universe without my volition—came and found a loving mother's arms to receive me. I had nothing to do with the preparation for my reception here. I have no power to change the environment of the future, but the same power which prepared the loving arms of a mother to receive me here will make proper reception for me there. God knows better than I what is good for me, and I leave it with God.

"If I had the power today by the simple turning of my hand to endow myself with personal immortality, in my infinite ignorance I would refuse to turn my hand. God knows best. It may be that there is a future life. I know that sometimes I get very tired of this life. Hedged and crippled, caged like a bird caught from the wilds, that in its mad desire for freedom beats its wings against the bars only to fall back in defeat upon the floor—I long for death, if it will but break the bars that hold me captive.

"I was snowbound in the mountains once for three days. On account of the snow we had to remain immediately alongside the train. After three days of this, when our food had been exhausted, the whistle blew that meant the starting of the train out into the world again. It may be that death is but the signal whistle that marks the movement of the train out into the broader stretches of spiritual being.

"As we stand in the presence of death, we have no knowledge, but always, no matter how dark the gloomy clouds hang before me, there gleams the star of hope. Let us hope, then, that it may be the morning star of eternal day. It is dawning somewhere all the time. Did you ever pause to think that this old world of ours is constantly swinging into the dawn? Down the grooves of time, flung by the hand of God, with every revolution it is dawning somewhere all the time. Let this be an illustration of our hope. Let us believe, then, that in the development of the human soul, as it swings forward toward its destiny, it is constantly swinging nearer and nearer to the sun.

"And now the time has come to say good-by. The word 'farewell' is the saddest in our language. And yet there are sentiments sometimes that refuse to be confined in that word. I will say 'Good-by, old man.' We will try to exemplify the spirit manifested in your life in bearing the grief at our parting. Words fail me here. Let these flowers, Riley, with their petaled lips and perfumed breath, speak in beauty and fragrance the sentiments that are too tender for words. Good-by."

FROM the time of the mountain men, who began their tales with "this old hoss reckons" and punctuated their stories with the grunted "wagh!" in imitation of the grizzly, Westerners have spoken a language flavored with their own words, words drawn from cattle, mining, and frontier life. Many of the words have passed into the American language, others are known throughout the West, and still others are pure localisms.

Men of the mining country spoke of *strikes, lucky strikes,* and *striking it rich.* They hit *pay dirt,* and when the ore was very rich, they were in *bonanza.* When they could find no *color* or when the vein *pinched out,* they were digging *country rock* and were working in *borrasca.* They *jumped claims* and *highgraded* the ore, stealing rich chunks of gold-bearing quartz, or *highgrade,* from tunnel *faces* that looked like *jewelers' shops.* Lunch buckets often left the mines heavier than when they were carried in. And one sanctimonious miner always carried a Bible to work with him, and amassed a small fortune filling its hollowed pages with rich ore. To protect themselves from miners who loaded their pockets and bulged their shirts with ore so heavy they could hardly waddle, mine owners introduced the *change room,* requiring miners to strip off their work clothes and change into street clothes before leaving the mine. Often there were two rooms with an intervening shower, and the miners walked naked from one to another, eliminating the possibility of transferring *highgrade* from overalls to suits.

Hardrock men, when they placed the stamp of approval upon a newcomer, observed, *Sure, he assays O.K.,* or *He'll assay.* When the new arrival was a disappointing *specimen,* when he didn't *pan out,* they dismissed him with, *He doesn't show the color,* or *I panned him down to bedrock and never struck pay dirt.* The hardrock men were quite generally contemptuous of "Johnny-Come-Latelies" who knew nothing of the mines or work in the mines. There was often good reason for the contempt, because the ignorance of the *farmer* frequently contributed to accidents. And many of these greenhorns actually were farmers, cowboys, or lumberjacks who worked in the fields and on ranches during the summer and supplemented their wages by work in the mines in winter. This half-and-half work was frowned upon by the year-round miner, who coined a variety of expressions for the outsider.

In Utah, the miners called them *hay hands, beet stopers, cow county boys, hay barbers, down homers, beet toppers, carrot pickers,* and *valley boys.* "You're no mountain man. What part of the valley do you come from?" In Montana and Idaho, they are more frequently referred to as *lumberjacks* and *spud pickers,* and also as *punkin rollers, alfalfa pickers,* and *apple knockers.* Arizona miners call them *cowboys, hay shovelers,* and *stubble jumpers.* Itinerant workers who wander over the Sierra from California are termed *prune pickers, orange pickers,* and, contemptuously, *Californians.* Miners delight also in riling the sensitive natures of the cockier West Coasters with the recitation of a rough but pointed quatrain, the rendition of which usually precipitates a certain amount of bottle throwing and chair banging:

> The miners came in '49,
> The whores in '51,
> They jungled up together
> And made the Native Son.

When the men were broke or hard up, they referred to the vein while speaking of themselves, *Yeah, she's pinching a bit.* And in desperate straits, *Why, man, I couldn't make money falling down a shaft at $8.50 a foot!*

They had specialized terms. Before the passage of safety laws governing the mines, the *chippy cage* in the shaft picked up anything—men, tools, ore. But the *chippy,* with its violent accidents passed. The picks, drills, and tools, protruding outward at an angle or flat on the bottom of the cage, struck the sides of the shaft as the cage was raised at terrific speed, hundreds of feet a minute. The men caught in it were literally churned to death, and the cage rose, a mass of mangled flesh at the surface. *Widow makers* were the early compressed-air drills creating the dust which caused silicosis. And a miner with silicosis had *rock on the chest, rock on the box, the miner's con* or, succinctly, *the miner's.* The *hush* in a mining camp was something more dreadful even than the wail of all the mine whistles screaming the warning of fire in the mine. The whistles, like air-raid sirens during the war, chilled everyone in camp. But the hush was more ominous and ghostly. Accustomed to the noise of the mine workings, the hoist motors, occasional blasting, and all the accepted sounds of a normal workday in a mining camp, there comes occasionally—silence. "Do you hear it? Hear the *hush?*" It meant at least something wrong in the mines, something not going smoothly as it should. Often it was the portentous omen of cave-in and disaster.

Cowboys were once *cowboys,* but as drugstore and dude have appropriated the title, it is being discarded on the range for the more specific *puncher, cowpoke, waddy,* and *wrangler.* The *cowpuncher* was originally the somewhat scorned individual who merely prodded and poked the cattle up the chute from the loading corral into the railroad cattle cars, but the term has moved back from town to the range. *Cowpoke* had a similar origin. The *wrangler's* job was the herding of horses, and the *waddy* was an extra hand hired at roundup time, "wadding" out the rancher's needs.

Among the cowboys, the expert horsemen bragged that they never *pulled leather* or *grabbed the apple,* holding on to the saddlehorn on a rough horse. The *top screw* was chief foreman of an outfit—anything was an *outfit,* from the whole ranch to a cowboy's possessions—and the *top hand* was an all-around good puncher, the best on the ranch. Cowboys rode *broncs,* branded *mavericks,* and

herded the *dogies*. *Line riders* rode the imaginary
line separating ranches, turning back unwanted
cattle, checking on stock, and also repairing the
drift fences along which cattle moved. A *grub-line
rider* scrounged free food traveling from ranch to
ranch, but the working cowboy came in at the end
of a roundup day to the *chuckwagon*. *Grub* was his
food and *java* his coffee, and instead of butter he
used *lick*, or syrup, on flapjacks and biscuits; the
cosi—from the Spanish *cocinero*—kept him well-
fed with steak and stew. After eating, the cowboy
relaxed with the *makings*, rolling a smoke with
cigarette papers from his *prayerbook* and tobacco
from his Bull Durham *sack*. He slept at the *bunkhouse* or, on the range, under a *sougan*, a small,
thick-woven blanket.

When a cowboy was utterly destitute, it was said
of him that he had *sold his saddle*. The term was
also one of contempt for the cowboy who had dis-
graced himself in some manner and been ordered
to *roll his bed* and *hit the trail*.

From Mexico the cowboys of the border borrowed terms which eventually reached the whole
West. *Chaps* came from *chaparejos*, *lasso* from *lazo*,
ranch from *rancho*, and *calaboose* from *calabozo*.
Unchanged were *vaquero*, *riata*, *sombrero*, *arroyo*,
bosque, *remuda*, and *rodeo*. The often repeated
words of greeting and farewell were quickly
adopted, the shortened *buenos*, the *adiós*, and *hasta*

mañana. An occasional *vaya con Diós*—"Go with God"—is heard. And the Southwesterner can scarcely pass a day without the casual use of *adobe, siesta, agua, mesa, pronto, río, hombre, hacienda, frijoles, tacos,* and *tequila.* From the Arabic into Spanish came *algodón;* the article *al* was dropped to give Arizona the word *cotton. Alfalfa* remained intact via the same route.

Spanish and Mexican curses, always the first words learned by the untutored linguist, passed rapidly into the Southwest. Blasphemous, horrifying, and electric in their effect when used by a group of Mexicans, their very strangeness and foreignness softened them on the lips of cowboys, who practiced them among themselves almost as academic exercises—the *sum, es, est, sumus, estis, sunt* of the open range. The cowboy's scholarly attainments, however, were often misunderstood—or too well understood—by the Mexican within hearing, and he showed his appreciation of the mastery of his language with knife and gun.

Less complicated, however, than the long curses were the brief *gringo* and *greaser.* Both have passed into the language of the West. Internationally understood, they contribute to no amity; both can be bitter and fight-provoking words. Even their origin is a matter of dispute. Some have claimed that Mexicans corrupted *green grow* into *gringo* from Burns's song which was popular with border troops:

> Green grow the rushes-oh,
> Green grow the rushes-oh,
> The sweetest hours that e'er I spend
> Are spent among the lasses-oh!

A more reasonable explanation is that the words *Es griego*—for "That's Greek"—were applied by Mexicans to denote the unintelligible speech of Americans and, as the Greek *barbaros,* for "foreigner," changed its meaning in English to become the scorned "barbarian," so *griego* along the border became, through malpronunciation, the slurring and contemptuous *gringo.* Similarly, *greaser* seems not to have come from any greasy appearance of the Mexicans—although that etymology is popular—but from the early days when a *greaser* actually ran beside the ox carts and great wagons with a bucket of tallow to oil the creaking, dry wheels. The procedure was something new to the first Americans, who remarked on the *greaser* at his work and, in time, adopted the now dubious term for all Mexicans.

When cowboys went to a Miles City ball, they *rode herd on the heifers* and *cut out* and *ran their brands* on the ones of their liking. At Santa Fe, the early tappers and traders took in the *fandangos* and courted the *señoritas.* They bought baubles and gimcracks, *forforraw*—from the Spanish *fanfarron* and French *frou-frou*—for their ladies and for themselves. They paid for their purchases with *plew*—beaver skin, from the French traders' *plus, plus,* "more, more"—and with *oro* dust, *dinero,* and *bit* pieces. The Westerner still reckons his purchases in *bits*—*two bits* to the quarter, *four bits* to the half dollar—and prefers the solid sound of coin, his *cartwheel* dollars, to the less tangible paper. When they were married, they got *hitched,* and when they were divorced, they *took the cure.*

The Westerner rarely "died." Nor was the problem of death a matter about which he talked other than casually. Of cowboys, it was said that they *had gone over the Divide, gone West* or *gone over the range.* Miners had *thrown dirt from the last ditch* or *gone up the flume.* They *gave up the game for good, passed in their checks, played their last cards,* or *drew to the spade.* More simply, it was said of a man that he *turned on his back* or *went under.* They often succumbed to *galena poisoning* or *lead poisoning.* The funeral service was a *send-off* and the burial itself a *planting.*

These words were generally and widely understood.

But occasionally there appears on the linguistic scene a gentleman like the scholarly and Oxford Spooner, who, as the result of his special and peculiar mangling of the language, adds his own name to it. A fair example of a spoonerism was the professor's statement to his students that he had pedaled to class on a "well boiled icicle." And also that there was much to be said for the poetry of "Sheets" over that of "Kelly." So that when certain Westerners in the mining camps of Montana and Nevada heard Earl Mullen speak, they began collecting his phrases and designating them "mullenisms." They were not malapropisms, such as those practiced by a Denver lady who spoke very seriously of purchasing "sexual bookcases" and who defended the largesse and public spirit of a Commissioner of Parks by stoutly referring to him as "one of the greatest philanderers in Colorado." Mullen's attack on the language was much more complicated than Mrs. Malaprop's confusion of single words or Spooner's simple transposition of letters.

Earl was a boomer, an Irish miner. He claimed to have known Jack London and to have received, in a barroom brawl in which both he and London participated, a knock on the head from a chair wielded by the West Coast author. It was this contact with literature, perhaps, which accounted for Mullen's generosity with the language, a generosity startling to the uninitiated and often surprising to Earl himself.

His departure from a bar was never a simple

matter. It required a flourish: "I shall beget myself over the threshold" or, when his steadiness had been questioned, "I shall carry myself forth to my utmost gentlemanship." When he saw a woman fumbling in her purse for a cigarette, he met the crisis with a startling, "Keep your portmanteau in silence. Here is a cigarette." On one occasion, when dullness had descended on the bar he was patronizing, he came out with a loud and commanding, "Let's have cul-de-sac!" John Kelly, bartending, stared openmouthed. Earl expanded his remark: "Let's have cul-de-sac! Let's go on a tear, get drunk!" Kelly said, "You don't know from your elbow what cul-de-sac means." Mullen, who never admitted to being trapped, explained, "I knew it didn't mean that. I was applying something in my misthoughted manner. It's French and it means to fight a duel." Everett Kinney, an old-timer who had been following the proceedings intently, threw the final monkey wrench into that conversation: "What sort of a coal sack are you talking about?"

Of death, he calmly asserted, "Defunctness is odiferous." When he saw another miner enjoying a sandwich, he left him slack-jawed with, "It's well devoured with ravishness and barbaric."

And when he had difficulty making out the scribblings of a note-taker, he asked, "What are you writing, English or Sanskrit?" He was told that it was English, but refused to believe it. "It looks more like eroglyphics."

"Eroglyphics?"

"Certainly. That's like the Sermon on the Mount definèd on the tombstones when Moses received the ovation from the skies."

NOT WELL, but hearty. Any advocate of a balanced diet would have had triple fits on the frontier.

There was, to begin with, the game of the trappers, the boudins and fat hump of the buffalo, the tongue and liver, delicacies eaten raw by the hungry men of the fur companies. And, while the game lasted, antelope and deer in the early settlements at four cents a pound, duck and wild turkey, fish and grouse.

When the great herds of game were gone, when the wanton trapping and killing had ended, there was the beef from the trail herds moving north out of New Mexico and Arizona into the rich country of Wyoming, Idaho, and Montana, the "heap beef" of the Indian who preferred a belly-filling meal of beef to a twenty-dollar gold piece, the beef of the cowpuncher and cattleman who butchered a calf a day when riding the range. "Sometimes it would be every other day, but mostly every day. When we got short of good fat calves, then we'd butcher dry cows, and sometimes it would be a big fat steer. Beef, just as good beef as we could get, and we had the best in the herd, too. There were usually ten to fifteen men in our range outfit, so it took a whole animal a day."

In the mining camps as well, once the trails and roads were opened to them, fresh meat was the most plentiful and least expensive food. As late as 1910, in out-of-the-way and almost inaccessible camps, top sirloin and New York cuts sold for ten cents a pound. In the Colorado camps the daily staple was beef, and in Central City, when other items were scarce, there was always the beef from the newly arrived oxen which had wearily and patiently hauled supplies across the plains. In the remote camps of Idaho and Montana, men lived

almost entirely on beef, varying the diet with
game and fish brought in by the Indians. And
when a guest in an Arizona restaurant complained
that he had been given beefsteak when he had
ordered mutton chop, the waiter replied, "Eat it,
you damned tenderfoot, or I'll wear it out on you!"

In addition to the beef and wild game available,
the two other basic staples on the frontier were
sourdough bread and baked beans. These were aug-
mented by salt pork, canned and dried fruits, canned milk, potatoes, onions, flour, coffee, sugar, salt,
and pepper. Beyond these, nothing. There was
little variation here, and the best that a good cook
could do was to come up with a stew or hash as a
change for the men, or with a Cousin Jack pasty
and potato pancakes. To the miner and cowboy,
however, the test of the food was not quality—in
terms of unusual and varied dishes—but quantity.
Good, solid food and plenty of it fully satisfied him.
A newcomer from the East, however, unable to for-
get the varied and succulent dishes of Pennsylvania, wrote that "dried apples are a necessary evil,
and canned peaches have become a byword and
an abomination." What was even more astonishing
to the Easterners was the fact that on a range with
twenty thousand head of cattle, there was not one
milk cow, and that the cowboys were content to
ride into town for their supply of canned milk.

There were no fresh vegetables, and the heavy

and unvarying diet—morning, noon, and night—
of beans, beef, and bread frequently brought on
scurvy, particularly in the mining camps, where a
good portion of the population was not as active
as the miners themselves or as the cowboys on the
range. The only, yet most certain, cure for scurvy
in the mines was a diet of raw potatoes soaked in
vinegar. Often the men were so absorbed with their
quest for gold that they improvidently laid no pro-
visions by for the winter. In Florence, Idaho, during the winter of 1861-1862, the miners were reduced to eating roots of plants and the inner bark
of trees.

In Arizona and New Mexico, on the other hand,
the Americans were introduced to a wide variety
of Indian-Mexican cookery, and the *cocinero* on
the cattle range was more apt to be a top Mexican
hand than an American. Indigenous cookery in
the Southwest is properly termed Indian-Mexican
rather than the often heard, but inaccurate, Spanish. The Spaniards of Spain, for example, do not
have *tacos, enchiladas, tamales, panocha,* or the hot
chili dishes, while their substantial egg *tortilla*
bears no relation to the thin, flat corn *tortilla* of the
Mexican border. The Spanish *tortilla,* a heavy, solid
omelet made of eggs, potatoes, ham, onion, and
herbs, was brought to Colorado and Montana by the
Basque sheepherders, although some have claimed
that the eggs which reached Denver and the min-

ing camps were so "high" that the Denver omelet and Denver sandwich—now commonly called Western—were evolved locally out of self-defense, the eggs so heavily seasoned with peppers, spices, ham, and anything at hand that they ceased to be offensive.

The cowboys and early settlers found the Mexican pinto beans—*frijoles*, usually seasoned with hot peppers—and the ever-present *chili con carne*. When well-prepared, the accurately named *chili con carne* (*Chili-chili; chili con carne* = chili with meat; *chili con carne con frijoles* = chili with meat with beans) was a delicacy in its own right, not to be confused with the inaccurately named concoctions served by cheap beaneries across the land or purchased in cans from the corner grocery. The best New Mexican *chili con carne* was made from a quantity of lean pork cut into one-inch squares and boiled until tender in covering water containing sage, crushed garlic, and salt. When tender, the meat was removed from the liquid stock and fried in pure lard with the addition of *chili* powder, gauged to taste by experience, and two or three tablespoons of browned flour. The meat and mixture in the frying pan were then returned to the original stock and allowed to boil down to the consistency of a medium-thick soup, which was served by itself or with rice and beans on the side. *Chili con carne* of this kind formed the center for the popular *tamale*, made in New Mexico simply by rolling a small quantity—two or three ounces—of cornmeal dough around the *chili con carne*, then encasing the whole in corn husks and steaming until cooked.

The Americans also found *tortillas*, the staff of life among the Mexicans of the Southwest. Made of hand-ground blue cornmeal into round, thin, pancakelike bread, *tortillas* served at mealtime as pushers to scoop up the *frijoles*, which were then eaten, *tortilla* and all. They formed the base also for the hot *tacos*, *enchiladas*, and other dishes which are still the pride of the better restaurants serving Mexican food in Albuquerque, Santa Fe, and Denver. *Tacos* were made of fine *tortillas* half folded, filled with meat, and fried in deep fat. Withdrawn from the fat, the *taco* was then stuffed from the sides with chopped onions, green *chili-*pepper sauce, shredded lettuce, and grated cheese. *Enchiladas* consisted simply of *tortillas* dipped in *chili* sauce and piled one on top of another, like pancakes, with chopped onions and grated cheese sprinkled between the layers, the whole crowned with a fried egg. Both dishes were hot enough to start rivulets of perspiration down the gourmet's, and certainly the gourmand's, neck.

The names of other dishes were colorful: *trigo cocido con carne de cabrito, arroz con pollo, chilis rellenos, albondigas, sopaipillas, adobado, mecha-*

dos, quesadillas, empanadas, panocha, and *pastel-litos.* And back of the names and the dishes lay the added color of New Mexico: the long strings of red *chili* peppers hanging from the beans of adobe houses; the red and black ears of Indian corn; the primitive, outdoor ovens; the *metates* and stones for grinding the corn; the mountain wood hauled in heavy wagons to the villages of Chimayo and Cordova; the slow smoke rising from homes where the sills were painted blue to keep out all evil.

Without this indigenous cuisine in the north, the men of the mining camps and cattle ranges nevertheless developed foods which are honored and respected today and, when available, are offered to the visitor as "something of the country." Much of the fare was simple, but with the hunger that came from a day's work, with the mountain air, and the view from mountain cabin or ranch house, the dishes partook of the flavor of a Western Olympus —Montana ambrosia, Idaho nectar.

Rocky Mountain oysters, the "lamb fries" available at gelding time, were simply tossed into the ashes of an outdoor fire, like potatoes. When they popped, the ashes were scraped off and the "oysters," seasoned with hot sauce, eaten with a sourdough biscuit. With canned jellies on hand, the cook varied the sourdough diet by coiling a strip of the dough around a stick which he held over the campfire until done. When pulled off, the hollowed

twist was filled with jelly. Jerky, either jerked beef
or jerked venison, has been a favorite of the West
from Jim Bridger's and Uncle Dick Wootton's time
to the present. The meat was cut in inch-wide strips,
rubbed with salt, and hung in the sun to dry. It
was chewed on at any time of the day, and the
traveler always carried a supply with him. Son-of-
a-bitch stew had everything in it, the tongue, liver,
kidneys, heart, sweetbreads, lights, and brains of a
newly killed calf, plus potatoes, tomatoes, onions,
and anything else at hand. It was cooked slowly
in an iron kettle and was not considered good if the
cowboy could tell what was in it by the time it was
ready to serve.

The cowboy's cuisine was based on food at hand
and in a large measure remains so. He was not
familiar with nor interested in unusual imported
foods and tended to look askance at them. Unlike
the mining camps, with their mixed population,
the men of the cow towns and ranches were basi-
cally American in stock and lacked any experience
with the long traditions of foreign foods. Con Price,
an old-time cowboy and friend of Charlie Russell's,
happily illustrates this with a story about the arrival of a piece of Limburger cheese at Philbrook,
Montana:

"I believe it was the spring of 1889 we met at
Philbrook in the Judith Basin for the spring roundup, and a lot of the boys were celebrating at the

post office and store. The postmaster told us someone had sent him a piece of Limburger cheese
through the mail. He didn't know what to do with
it as he didn't know anyone civilized enough to eat
it, so he gave it to the cowboys, who put in a lot of
their time rubbing it on doorknobs, the insides of
hat bands, and drinking cups. They had the whole
town well-perfumed. Then someone noticed an old-
timer who had come to town to tank up on joy juice
and had got so overloaded he went to sleep in the
saloon. His heavy drooping mustache gave one of
the boys an idea. A council was held and it was
agreed that he should have his share of the Limburger rubbed into his mustache under his nose.
Being unconscious, old Bill slept like a baby in a
cradle while the work was done.

"Next day Charlie Russell saw him out back of
the saloon, sitting on a box and looking very tough.
He would put his hands over his mouth, breathe into
them, drop them and look at them, and shake his
head. Of course, Charlie knew what was the trouble
as he had helped to fix him up the night before.
Charlie went over to him and asked, 'How are you
stacking up today?' Old Bill looked at him in a kind
of daze and shook his head. 'Me? I'm not so good.'
Charlie asked, 'What's the matter, are you sick?'
'No-o-o, not more than usual, I've felt as bad as
this a thousand times. But—oh God . . .' Then he
covered his face again with his hands. After a few

seconds he slowly lowered them, shaking his head and groaning, 'Oh, it's something awful, I don't savvy.'

"Charlie, very much in sympathy with him, said, 'What seems to be the matter, Bill?' 'Damned if I know, but I've got the awfulest breath on me. 'Pears like I am plum spoiled inside. You can tell the boys my stay here on earth is damn short. Nobody could live long with the kind of breath I've got on me. Oh, oh!' Then he would breathe into his hands again, saying, 'Oh God!'

"I believe he would have died if they hadn't told him what was the matter."

In Butte, the mainstay of the Irish miners was "stirabout." This was no more than old-fashioned oatmeal thinned with milk, and was served by the ton to the miners. The Florence and Clarence Hotels, boardinghouses renamed the Big Ship and the Madhouse by the men, served several hundred miners daily, each of whom had three or four bowls as a starter for his meals. The cousin Jack pasty was made of the best tenderloin or sirloin meat diced into cubes and, with diced potatoes and seasoning, wrapped in pie-crust dough and cooked in the oven. The result was a tasty meat-pie turnover that kept hot for hours, and when the Cornishman found one in his lunch bucket, he called it "a letter from home." Saffron bread and saffron buns were traditional with the Cornish, also, as were their oaten cakes and the potato pancakes well flavored with caraway seeds served on Christmas Eve. In Idaho, cush was a favorite dish made of cornbread crumbs, butter, salt, pepper, and enough water to give the whole the consistency of stuffing. This was fried in hot butter and eaten at breakfast, lunch, and dinner.

But as the camps grew into towns and cities, and as wealth poured out of the mines, the men were not limited in their choice of food to what the country alone could provide or to what they themselves could cook. The great hotels came into being—the Windsor in Denver; the Hotel de Paris in Georgetown, Colorado; the International Hotel in Virginia City, Nevada; and the Hotel de France in Lewiston, Idaho—which served dinners equal to any found in the country. The railroad made the importation of delicacies easy, and menus overflowed with oysters, lobsters, shrimp, and seafoods; with caviar, *pâté de foie*, and other rarities from Europe; with fresh fruits and vegetables from the region itself or from California; and with wines that would have done credit to New York or Paris. Elk, venison, and beef were prepared with Continental recipes. Times changed and the cooks were Italian, German, and French chefs. One of them, Louis du Puy, owner of the Hotel de Paris, left his mark not only in the West but upon the country as a whole. The late Dean James E. Russell of Columbia's Teacher's College, visiting the West, was so impressed with du Puy's cuisine and with the Frenchman's comments on the relation of good food to the well-being of individual and home that he introduced at Columbia the first domestic science courses in the United States. Today, while much of the food is still imported, the West itself has begun to ship its own delicacies to the country. Irrigation has wrought the change in some sections, making Arizona dates and grapefruits, the Fallon turkeys and canteloupes of Nevada, and the Pascal celery of Colorado prime items on Eastern menus. The potatoes of Idaho are, of course, a byword.

THE Westerner is a confirmed prospector. To-day, when he stops his car by the side of the road, he will pick up rock, look at it, weigh it, and guess at its nature before chucking it away for another. It is done almost aimlessly, without prefigured method or purpose. The act comes as naturally to him as crawling does to a child or exploratory osculation to a teen-ager. It is part of his being, inherited from his ancestors on the land, inherited

from the land itself. Unless he is a geologist, there
is little promise for him. But he has heard the stories of lucky strikes and knows that part of the West
grew from its mines. So he goes through the mo-
tions of his predecessors, the men who once roamed
the land with burro and grubstake, the men who
hunked down close to the earth to gaze hopefully
at quartz float, or who studied the broken formation of gulch outcroppings.

Even the newcomer picks and pokes at the rock,
striving to understand its mysteries. As he does so,
he becomes kin to the prospector. The land is silent
around him, quiet, and the sun burns the distances.
It is desolate, empty. Yet on this barren hillside or
on that vast, dry plain, there may be an "indication," a sign of precious metal. And back of the surface showing, there may be a great ledge of gold
or silver-bearing ore. The lone prospector's act of
picking up a single rock, his shrewd judgment of
its worth, may bring into being a brawling, lusty
city in the middle of nowhere—a Bisbee, a Ouray,
a Frisco, a Hamilton.

The great majority of the Western mines were
found not by knowledgeable perseverance alone or
by chance alone, but by a happy combination of
both. Just as the research student or scholar has
stumbled on a "lucky" bit of proof in his work, so
the prospector made his "lucky" strike. But neither
would have made their finds without a background

of training which gave each the power of recognizing values when seen, or without an objective toward which each was striving. How many researchers have passed over, without awareness, secrets of unmeasured value to wiser colleagues? How many men have walked the land of the West and seen gold, silver, and copper outcroppings without knowing their worth?

The "desert rats," the nonbookish scholars of the land, were a clan unto themselves. And what motivated them? Why should a man wish to depart into the desert for weary months, alone, with only a patient burro as companion, and all his worldly possessions—begged or borrowed—a sack of beans, water cans, a blanket, a pick, and shovel? He was supported by a variety of reasons. First, he was an explorer and he loved the land. There was pride in knowing that he was the *first* to explore this mountain range, to find this spring, to come upon that valley. Second, the hunt itself was exciting. The gold or silver was there, still is there, to be found. There was no doubt of its existence, only the question of interpreting the treasure map, the land. And third, what if the prospector should find it? What then? Why, he would have a secret to himself for which all men hungered. He would know! He would come plodding out of the desert with his burro, a lone man, ragged, bearded, hungry, the butt of jokes. But tomorrow, ah, tomorrow, who would then have money to throw at the birds? Who would then be praised for foresight and wisdom? Why, the prospector! The mirage was always on the horizon. Just over that ridge, perhaps; up that ravine, maybe . . .

And so these men—many of whom were to die in the desert, many of whom were to grow insane with unrealized visions—opened the mineral West.

In 1899, Jim Butler headed south from his ranch at Belmont toward the newly discovered Southern Klondike diggings, fourteen miles south of Tonopah, named by the Indians for "little water." He prospected the country without success until one morning he awoke to find his burro missing and started out on a prolonged search for the animal. Butler finally located it standing patiently behind a ridge. Legend has it that Butler picked up a rock to throw at the animal and that just as he was about to hurl it, he saw glistening ore in his hand. Actually, he sat down by an outcropping ledge to rest and, true to his prospector instincts, chipped away at the rock. Returning home, he sent the specimens to a friend, Tasker L. Oddie, who, in turn, passed them on to an assayer in Austin. The assayer's eyes bugged out when his tests showed the ore running between eight hundred and a thousand dollars a ton. Some little time passed before Butler got around to staking claims (he had haying to do!), but when he finally located them, the rush was on that was to unearth $125,000,000 in gold and silver. In Tonopah today, the favorite postcard of all is the one of Butler and his burro, captioned with a quote from the small, patient animal: "Me and Jim found Tonopah."

Jokingly referred to as the "desert canary," "Rocky Mountain Canary," or "Washoe canary," maligned, castigated, overburdened, beaten, the little burro was, nevertheless, the forerunner of all transportation on the desert and in the high mountain gulches. He was the alter ego of the prospector, and without him many a mining camp would still be a sagebrush flat or an unknown ravine. The Denver artist, Herndon Davis, honored him with several drawings and with a water color titled "Sir Burro"—a head in profile, surmounted by the crest of the State of Colorado and signed by Governor Ralph Carr. The town of Fairplay buried the sixty-two-year-old Prunes—a burro that had worked in every mine of the Fairplay-Alma district from 1867 to 1929—under a monument erected by the citizens in 1930. And Robert Sherwood, an old-time miner, was buried at his own request besides Prunes. Cy Warman gave the burro a prominent and deserved place in his brief poem on the roaring, round-the-clock camp of Creede:

> Here's a land where all are equal,
> Of high or lowly birth,

A land where men make millions,
Dug from the dreary earth.
Here the meek and mild-eyed burro
On mineral mountains feed—
It's day all day in the daytime,
And there is no night in Creede.

The cliffs are solid silver,
With wond'rous wealth untold,
And the beds of running rivers
Are lined with glittering gold.
While the world is filled with sorrow,
And hearts must break and bleed—
It's day all day in the daytime,
And there is no night in Creede.

The burro and the prospector hunted together. But in the folklore of the mining camps, there were other helpers and mines were found in other varied ways. Prospectors have always checked the dirt and pebbles thrown up by burrowing animals, badgers, gophers, and rabbits. In Eureka, Utah, ore containing horn silver and worth a dollar a pound was found in gopher holes. Mines have been located when cattle on the trail have chipped surface rock to disclose the presence of gold. A sheepherder, riding through a narrow pass near Fish Springs in Juab County, Utah, chanced to strike his stirrup against rock which broke and glistened in the sun. A cowboy in Nevada was thrown from his horse— not into sagebrush or tumbleweed, but into a body of rich ore which turned him from a puncher into a millionaire. The wheels and hubs of heavy wagons have crushed rock and uncovered gold and silver. And prospectors who have hunted in vain for precious ore have disgustedly thrown their tools down—to strike it. The Shoebridge Bonanza Mine in Utah was discovered in this fashion by a prospector who threw his pick away. As it hit the ground, it turned up a rich vein of silver.

Related to this last-minute accidental finding of gold and silver is the tradition of the "last round." Many a miner has sunk a prospect shaft or tunnel only to find continuing borrasca. Disappointed, he has sold out cheaply or left the claim to the next comer. And the first round fired by the second owner has brought in "bonanza." "One more round for luck" has become custom, linked to the saying,

> Stick and stay,
> God damn, we'll make her pay!

Miners and prospectors had little use for forked sticks and doodlebugs in their hunt for treasure. "I got hold of one of the contraptions and it went bz-z-z bz-z-z and led me straight to a horseshoe." But some credence was given, by Snowshoe Thompson at least, to Eilley Orrum's claim that she had located a vast body of ore near Sun Mountain with her old cloudy "peep stone." "If I could only get a new peep stone, I could locate it exactly." But Sacramento shops were not stocking peep stones, so the Comstock had to wait for O'Riley and Mc-Laughlin. In Utah, where Brigham Young at first forbade prospecting for gold and silver, preferring to build his society on a stable, agricultural base, mines were ultimately located as the result of prophetic dreams. These "dream mines," sanctioned by the Church, were often developed at great expense only to prove barren and nonproductive. The Mormons have kept the workings open, however, some of them believing that when a great crisis affects the land, then the mines will produce fabulously and save the Church and her people.

Once gold and silver had been discovered in a region, the surrounding area was ripe for prospectors, the majority of them greenhorns who stumbled on strikes virtually by accident. In 1892, James Burns and James Doyle, for want of anything better, staked the only bit of unclaimed land in Victor, Colorado, a small piece scarcely one-sixth of an acre in size. They borrowed a clothesline to claim and mark off their property. Digging, they at first struck only country rock and, lacking funds, offered a third interest in their "mine" to Johnny Harnam, another Irishman, for $300. With this small capital they worked ahead into extraordinarily rich ore, the great bed of the $65,000,-000 Portland Mine. Similarly, John Bernard, who knew nothing of prospecting and who had walked to the same district from Colorado Springs, staked an area topped by an ordinary pile of rocks, a place considered worthless. He had located a mine which produced $13,000,000, a half interest in which he had sold to two grocers as settlement for a $36.40 food bill. And in Butte, a prospector who had met with no luck decided to quit his wandering and turn to the hotel business. He purchased a lot in the center of town upon which the small Smoke House cigar store stood. This he tore down and, grumbling at the expense, blasted a ledge of rock for his cellar and foundation. When the smoke cleared, he gazed at a twenty-five-foot ledge of peacock copper.

There are stories also current in the camps of greenhorns who were jokingly advised to dig in the most unlikely spots—under pine trees or high on a ravine where all experience had shown the ore to be at creek level—and who confounded the jokesters by turning up rich diggings. Haw Tabor, in Colorado, was "skinned" when he was maliciously sold a barren mine for $17,000. It produced as many millions. And Bummer Dan, in Virginia City, Montana, was ordered by long-suffering miners to go to work or to leave camp. Accepting the horrible fate, he was assigned a digging on a bar about a mile from the main strike. Here, working alone, he turned up several thousands of dollars in gold and gave his name to Bummer Dan's Bar.

Gold is where you find it, and the axiom is nowhere more clearly illustrated than in the ever recurrent tale of the funeral service preached beside an unfinished grave, the corpse suddenly forgotten when gravediggers and mourners sighted rich ore. The preacher, a man of frontier vision, rose quickly to the occasion and cut the sermon short with a hasty and practical, "Amen! Boys, stake me out a slice of that!"

Lost mines were a natural corollary to those which had been discovered and worked. There are more than four hundred such mines in the West and, unlike the fish that got away, most have been authenticated to the extent at least that persons other than the discoverer saw proof of the precious ores. The reasons for their being lost are varied and yet obvious. The discoverer of vast wealth was often secretive, and knowledge of the location of a mine passed with his death—a death which might be natural, but which was more often due to starvation and thirst in the desert or the result of avaricious murder. Again, the original discoverer of ore was often unaware of the value of his find until an assay had proved it, and more often than not neglected to mark its location adequately upon discovery. Lastly, the land itself changed, with winter storms, avalanches, and landslides hiding forever the briefly discovered wealth.

The Lost Mine of Hicks Mountain—actually never worked as a mine—was discovered in 1895 by Douglas McLean, a tenderfoot who had come to Colorado for his health. Rabbit hunting in the late fall, he entered the dense timber of Mount Bergen on the side closest to Hicks Mountain. Here he became hopelessly lost and wandered until dusk, when he saw an outcropping ledge of rose quartz, eighteen feet wide. He chipped some specimens from it and eventually made his way to the Witter Ranch and from there to Evergreen. The assays of the quartz, full of coarse gold, ran $1000 to the ton, but heavy snows prevented McLean's immediate return to the spot, and his efforts to find it again in the two succeeding years failed. McLean stated that the ledge was under an overhanging bank of earth, and it is quite probable that this caved with the spring thaws. He insisted, however, that the gulch, where the ledge still remains to be located, was either a branch of Witter Gulch or the next big gulch entering Bear Creek below Witter.

Similarly, members of a party of California emigrants in the Quinn River desert and Black Rock region of Nevada found loose lumps and heavy slabs of pure silver partially hidden under deep volcanic ash. The natural smelting process of volcanic fires had seemingly reduced the ore, pieces of which were so heavy that they could not be carried. With the goal of California before them, and beset by Indians and the hazards of the desert crossing, they pushed on across the Sierra. When men of the party returned in the '50's in an attempt to relocate the area, the place could not be found. Also, in northern Nevada, certain emigrants who were ignorant of the nature of gold were amused when the women and children of their party picked up pretty pebbles which they carried with them or tossed in the buckets hanging by the side of the wagons. The pebbles were pure gold, as Californians were to tell them, but the unknown ravine where hundreds more lay scattered on the ground was never rediscovered. A like fate befell the Lost Cabin Mine in the Big Horn country of Wyoming or Montana. Three prospectors had penetrated deep into the Sioux lands to find gold. Two of the men were killed by the Indians and the third, escaping with specimens of ore which are still spoken of with awe, was unable to retrace his route.

The shifting sands of the desert have taken their toll of legendary wealth. Near Quartzsite, Arizona, the superintendent of a mine became lost in a desert sandstorm, driven before the swirling, biting dust until he found refuge behind a quartz ledge on the desert floor. When the storm had passed, he saw that the quartz was full of free gold. Breaking off samples, he stuffed them in his pocket and marked his claim to the ledge by leaving his coat and six-shooter upon it. From where he could observe the surrounding mountains, he also described as best he could, in a notebook, the location of the ledge. But weakened as he was by storm and thirst, he never reached town. Search parties found him dead in the desert. The ore samples assayed $25,000 to the ton, but what the desert unearthed in storm it as quickly covered again. The ledge remains lost.

The names of the mines are enough in themselves to lure the seeker, and the word "lost" is an invitation: the Lost Soldier and Lost Shovel of Wyoming; the Lost Adam's Diggings, the Lost Dutchman and the Lost Mines of Tumacacori in Arizona; the Lost Blue Bucket and the Lost Diamond in Nevada; and the Juan Carlos Lost Mine of the San Luis Valley, the Breckenridge Huntsman Lost Mine, and the George Skinner Lost Mine of Wet Mountain Valley in Colorado.

Death lies in back of many of them, waiting then, as now, for the foolhardy hunter, the man overconfident in the desert, the prospector once too gold-loco to heed warnings of Apaches. The two Frenchmen who found the Lost Penhachape Mine never did return to Yuma, where they had purchased their supplies with ore of marvelous quality in 1869. The Apaches killed all the miners working the Lost Don Miguel Peralta Mine in the Superstition Mountains east of Phoenix; and the Lost Dutchman—which may have been the Peralta mine rediscovered by Jacob Walz—was stained with later blood. But the mines and diggings are still there—some hidden and camouflaged by their long-dead discoverers, others buried by Nature—

and are still the subject of search. The Phoenix Dons make an annual pilgrimage hunting for the treasure of the Superstitions, and single prospectors still pack into the desert looking for "indications," seeking to find what was lost.

BELOW and aboveground, the Western miner holds to his superstitions and his customs. On the great mining circle followed by boomer and ten-day miners, the traditions circulate by word of mouth from one man to another, until today, in any going camp, the hardrock driller or lowly mucker will be familiar with them all and practice at least some. They stem in many cases from old wives' tales, but some have the bedrock of common sense behind them.

Anyone who has gazed down the deep shaft of a mine dropping thousands of feet into the earth, or walked even a few feet into a tunnel piercing the heart of a mountain, needs no description of the feeling of awe and fear that the visitor experiences. This feeling is one shared by the men themselves, even by those miners who have worked years underground. The mine contains strange sounds: the dripping of water, the distant ring of a pick, the groan of timbers supporting tons of earth, the shifting of the earth, the scurry of rats. Sights in the mines are equally strange and disconcerting: shadows from miners' lights play curiously on the tunnel walls, ore formations create weird designs, ghostly lights from crosscuts and winzes flicker in the tunnels, and apparitions appear to the credulous or even the hardened miner.

There is danger and death in the mines. There is the slow death from silicosis, "the miner's." There is quick death—a horrifying fall thousands of feet down the shaft and a man's body brought up as small bits of flesh; a dropped steel falling from above and splitting a man in half; an unexploded round—a "missed hole" or "sleeper"—detonating unexpectedly; the cage lowered too far and the men drowning like rats in the watery sump at the bottom of the shaft; or a cage hoisted too rapidly to the surface and crushing the men to pieces against the hoist timbers. There are cave-ins, explosions, and that most dreaded disaster, fire in the mine. It is small wonder that the Cornish and Welsh miners descended to work singing "Nearer My God to Thee," and that all miners, while they joked about death, gave personal credence to omens of good and ill fortune.

There is mystery in the mine as well, the mystery of the moving earth. Two miners resting in a lonely tunnel deep in the mine, in the utter silence of the graveyard shift, feel and hear the light quake, the vibration, the groaning of the earth. A stranger would be terrified. One miner speaks casually to the other, "She's turning over"—the world turning on its daily axis and the burdened earth adjusting itself.

The miner's chief belief lay in his hunches. If it was not his "day" to go to work, he remained at home, forfeiting his pay. Many tales have corroborated the wisdom—or luck—of these hunches. Miners have been known to walk to the mouth of the shaft, then suddenly change their minds and return to the safety of home. Accidents have occurred on these days. Miners' wives have had premonitions and dreams about death and disfigurement, and the miner, not wishing to risk his luck, has remained aboveground. Where men have scoffed at the premonitions of their wives, the women have plied them with whisky and kept them drunk in order to protect them from danger. Even on shift men have changed their minds. Paddy Monohan started work one day at the Mayflower Mine in Silverton, Colorado, but suddenly said, "The sign ain't right," and quit the job on the spot. Two hours later, a slab came down and killed the man working in his place.

When accidents occurred in a mine, the wise miner left to rustle another job. Some miners stood for one close call, but quit after the second. The third was the fatal one. At the United States Mine in Bingham Canyon, Utah, a worker accidentally dropped a Leyner steel which half pierced a twelve-by-twelve timber. A miner, standing on the timber at the time, left the job immediately. He rustled work at the Highland Boy, but had another close call, and quit at once to go to work at the Delaware Copper. The basis in fact for this superstition is that when carelessness crops up in a mine, it makes good sense to get out. This carelessness may be due to the miner himself, who, after a time, takes one mine and its workings for granted. Conscious of his self-created danger, he quits and goes to another mine, where he approaches the work in a new, strange place more carefully.

Other warnings and omens which the miner took seriously included those relating to the "change room." When a hardrock miner's clothes slipped from their hook and fell to the floor, he looked upon the sign as one of very bad luck, portending his own fall in the mine. Similarly, in the mine itself, when a timber fell, the omen was bad. Some miners believed that good luck attended when they wore their oldest and dirtiest clothes while working; and to change clothes, once they had been put on, was bad luck. To wear a necktie in the mine was downright idiocy, and miners explained that any man wearing one "would be bad luck in person."

In all mining country, also, it was extremely bad luck to have a woman enter a mine. Miners quit the workings and refused to go back until she had left. In Mexico, this superstition was once carried to the point where miners refused to re-enter a mine until the local priest had come with holy water and, taking an elbow from the compressor supplying air, blown the purifying water throughout the whole workings. At the Rose Nicol Mine in Cripple Creek, a woman visited the tunnels one day in 1926. That same night there was an accident, and a week later a miner fell from the hoist bucket and was killed in the sump. Mike Cloney, mining at the Keystone in Gold Hill, said, "On the night before I got hurt, two women and two fellows came down to visit the mine. The foreman refused to let them go through the workings, but I and my partner, Wally Smol, insisted he let them go. The next night we had a cave-in." Cloney's leg was

crushed and a year later it had to be amputated
at the knee.

To state in advance the last day a miner intended
to work was to invite disaster. Miners rarely said,
"This is my last day, I'm quitting tonight." There
have been sufficient instances of accident and death,
coupled with the post-mortem talk of "Poor guy,
and on his last day . . ." to make the superstition
stick. To placate the fates, miners either said nothing about "last day" work until the shift was ended,
or advanced the actual date. "I'm quitting next
week." Then, with the last shift over, they washed
down in their favorite saloon their luck at avert-
ing death.

When a miner met death in the mine, however,
his fellow workmen left at once, without finishing
the shift, and frequently remained away for several days. Even when a miner died aboveground,
of the "con" or as the result of an accident, some
miners refused to return to work. This custom, one
of simple respect for the dead coupled with the fear
of death, has fallen out of practice more recently,
because a death in one working of a large mine
does not become known to men in distant workings
until hours later. Those miners near the dead man,
however, will leave.

There were widespread superstitions relating to
lights and candles in the mines. When a candle
went out three times or fell from the tunnel wall,

it was a sign to old-timers—particularly Cousin Jacks—that someone was at home with the wife. They at once left the mine to check on the carryings-on of the "old woman." To find three candles or lights in a mine drift at the same time was considered very bad luck, and a miner seeing two others blew out his own. There was the ready proverb, "If the candle goes out, you go out, too," referring to the fact that a candle will not burn in bad air. There was also the saying, "Always light your own candle. Never light one candle from another." At the Fairview Mine near Pitkin, Colorado, Matt Lannon refused to give a light from his candle to a miner whose own had gone out. The reason offered was, "It takes the life out of a candle to pass the light from one to another." A secondary and sensible reason was that "You've got to learn to do things for yourself in the mine. Suppose you were alone down here?"

It was, and is, an unwritten and traditional law among mining men never to strike a man underground. However incensed one miner may be with another, the invitation in the lower levels is always, "Come on out on the dump and settle it!" Pat Harrington, doublejacking at the Little Earl Mine near Tin Cup, joshed his partner, who was holding the drill. His partner replied, "Hell, even if you did hit my finger, it wouldn't hurt!" The insult was more than any self-respecting doublejacker—wielding an eight-pound hammer—could stand, and the invitation to go out of the mine followed. To fight in the mine itself, in the narrow space of the tunnel, with tools handy, was to invite serious personal injury as well as to endanger the safety of other miners.

Animals were generally credited with being helpful to the miner. When a newcomer to the mines was so foolish as to kill a rat, old-timers almost beat the life out of him, simply to teach him the lesson that what might be pests elsewhere were, in the mines, to be left alone, even pampered as pets. "When the rats leave, get out!" The animals seem to have a sixth sense about impending cave-ins, fires, and explosions, and the miners watch their actions carefully. The Copper Queen in Bisbee has an elaborate safety system for fires and other accidents, by which an unpleasant "stink" is blown through the compressor to all parts of the mine, warning the men of danger. Yet even before the smell has reached the workings, miners will have observed the nervous and peculiar actions of the rats around the timbers. The "stink" simply confirms their presentiment that something is wrong.

Mules were credited with this sixth sense also. Ed Webb, who worked twenty years ago at the Eagle Mine in Eureka, Utah, was loading muck when his mule started out of the tunnel before the car was filled. "I caught up with her and beat hell out of her, but just as I finished, the whole tunnel caved behind us. I took that mule out and gave her the best feed she ever had."

Prospectors, rather than miners, also befriended the friendly and curious jay—the "camp robber" or "camp robin"—and the porcupine. To kill either was to incur their wrath. The jay is an amusing bird, often providing the only companionship for many a lonely prospector, and men who have unwittingly injured a "camp robber" have gone to great lengths to care for the bird until it was well. The same held true for the pack rats, and some of the small animals were even credited with bringing ore specimens to the prospector in exchange for something else stolen. The porcupine was an animal almost sacred, a superstition which came into being quite practically. Because the porcupine is a slow-moving animal, the prospector who found himself in dire straits from hunger could easily catch one to provide needed food. They were killed only in case of absolute necessity.

Black cats carried their usual ill luck. In Virginia City, Steve Chopp started for the Hale and Norcross Mine, when a black cat crossed his path. He went to work with misgivings and, as luck would have it, drove a pick into his foot. He was laid up for a time, but again, on the third day after he had returned to work, he met another. Steve sat in the "change room" several minutes, debating whether to go down or return to his boarding-house. He finally decided to put in a day's work. Kelly, timekeeper and aboveground boss, said, "Damned if a piece of spiling didn't come down and knock him on the head. Steve quit for the day."

The 1,300-foot level—like the 13th floor of office buildings and hotels—was skipped in the number-ing sequence. And in the coal mines of Utah, "room" 13 was considered unlucky. Miners refused to cut the "room" and left the pillar of coal stand-ing. At the Kenilworth Mine in the same state, Tommy Gibbons had the 13 cleaned up except for a small amount of muck in one corner. As he stooped over, a piece of coal fell from the "ceiling" and broke his neck, killing him.

Whistling in a mine invariably brought bad luck, and old-time foremen summarily fired any offenders. Its immediate effect was to cause the "pinching out" of the ore, rendering work in the mine useless, but it also brought cave-ins and like disasters to the offender. To hear anyone whistling on the way to work was in itself bad luck for the miner.

A similar, curious belief among mining men of the last century was that "churches kill a camp." They did not mean that the civilizing influence of the church caused the suppression of saloons and gambling clubs, but that, in fact, when churches were built in a mining community, the mineral resources were actually spirited away, causing the ruin of the town. It was "as if the argentiferous deposits were the strong box of Pluto himself, who, upon the advent of the messengers of his Almighty Adversary, as if they were spies, decamped, taking his treasures with him." One mining man of education and wide experience claimed that in the Arizona camp where he was working in 1886 the yield of ore had fallen off fifteen per cent since the construction of the first church, and that "one more church would ruin the camp."

Tommy Knockers were the importation of English and Cornish miners, but their tradition is as old as the medieval legends of elves and gnomes. They have been variously described by Western miners as "little brown men" or "little men about two feet high," and some miners have expanded the description to include their clothes, little mining boots, and colored shirts. They were rarely seen, however, and their presence was known more by the sounds they made and by actions attributed to them. Miners believed that Tommy Knockers were friendly and playfully mischievous, but occasionally vindictive when they were mistreated or ignored.

Tommy Knockers usually worked in mines where high-grade ore was found, and miners who believed in them claimed that the little men, with their tapping, led them to rich veins. They also warned miners of impending danger. When Boswell Reed of Denver was camping with four other miners in Nevada, one of them rose suddenly from his bed and left the cabin, telling the others to leave also. When asked why, he replied that the Tommy Knockers had warned him. Turning back the bedclothes—since the miner would not return until everything had been inspected—the men discovered a large centipede. In the mines, also, when men heard the tap-tapping of the Tommy Knockers as they worked with pick and drill, they were at once fearful of danger. Unable to explain the sounds, other than to attribute them to the warning signals of the small workmen, they left the working rather than stay and court disaster and death. When Tommy Knockers were simply mischievous, they were blamed by the miners for hiding tools or scattering them through the workings, upsetting lunch buckets and otherwise making themselves a nuisance.

I'm a hardrock miner an' I ain't afeard o' ghosts,
But my neck-hair bristles like porcupine's quills,
An' I knock my knuckles on the drift set posts
When the Tommy Knockers hammer on the caps an' sills,
An' raise hallelujah with my picks an' drills!

Geologists and engineers, who were less credulous than the miner, attributed all the actions of the Tommy Knockers to natural causes. At night, in the silence of the mine thousands of feet below-ground, the slightest sound is magnified in the echoing tunnels. The drip of water on metal plate sounds like distant singlejacking, and the tap-tap-tap of a ghostly pick may be nothing more than the same water dripping on highly metallic ore. But to convince the miner of this was frequently impossible. They not only believed in the Tommy Knockers, but also attributed the ghostly drilling to the spirits of dead miners who continued working at the spot where they were killed or attempted to dig themselves out of caved tunnels. Miners gave a wide berth to the spots where fellow workmen met their death.

> Pick, pick, pick.
> Has someone behind us knocked?
> Pick, pick, pick.
> No, 'tis souls of dead miners locked,
> For they're locked in the earthen wall,
> Those that found death down there . . .
>
> And we leave the haunted place,
> For we won't work where they be,
> And wherever we hear them knocking
> We sure will always flee.
> For it means whoever hears it
> Will be the next in line,
> For the pick-pick of the Tommy Knockers
> Is the last and awful sign.

A STEER was not like any other piece of property upon which a man could lay his hands at will and which he could identify without trouble.

Of their own brute volition, on unfenced land, the animals wandered off the owner's range in search of greener grass and better water holes. They drifted before winter storms. They were the subject of raids by rustlers, organized outlaws driving hundreds of head to other country or an unscrupulous individual simply profiting from the chance opportunity of a moment to add a single animal to his own herd.

Cattlemen of the West, to identify their property and protect their rights, ran their hot irons upon the herd and branded their claim to ownership for all honest men to see and respect. Like the men who owned and named the mines, the owners of herds—large or small—designed and named their brands and left them for the history of the West.

Brands lived impermanently, for the lifetime of the cattle, upon hides. Where stock flourished and increased, the brands grew and were handed from generation to generation. Where cattle sickened and died, when drought or storm came to the land, when men failed, the brands died also.

Yet even where the brands have disappeared from the range, a partial record of them has been kept in registers and brand books. This was done haphazardly at first, locally and voluntarily, simply for mutual protection and information. Then, under the pressure of local custom and the outcome of disputes, the registering of brands became a matter of law, administered by each county. And finally, as the brands overlapped and gross and conscious similarities were found in the brands of bordering counties, an even more centralized authority became necessary. Today all brands are registered under the authority of each state with the various State Boards of Live Stock Commissioners, and the brands themselves published periodically in book form with supplements as needed.

With this centralization of authority, the further duplication of brands within a state is now prohibited, yet all those which were in use and found to be duplicates when they were first transferred from county records have been retained. There is, resultingly, some existing duplication in any given state, and much more if one eliminates state boundaries. But in terms of the total number of brands, the confusion created is negligible. It becomes of slight importance when it is realized, for example, that the S Bar S brand of Helen Thomas's ranch in Nevada is branded on the left shoulder and an identical S Bar S, as far distant as Fremont County, Wyoming, is registered as a brand on the right ribs. The location of the brands—shoulder, thigh, hip, ribs, neck, and jaw—was as carefully designated as the brand itself. A further distinction was made also between the location of the same brand on horses and cattle.

The number of brands runs into the tens of thousands. For the eight states which we are considering, there have been no fewer than one hundred thousand registered brands. Taking at random the official brand books of Wyoming, Colorado, Arizona, and New Mexico for different years, these astonishing figures appear: For the year 1907, the

Brand Book of the Territory of New Mexico listed more than 24,380 brands. Wyoming, for the year 1916, recorded approximately 14,400. Colorado claimed 23,250 in 1906. And for 1933, Arizona listed more than 7,360.

When one considers the brands which were never recorded and those which have been lost or destroyed, it is no exaggeration to estimate a total of at least three hundred thousand brands for the area.

The brand books, now rare and collectors' items except for those of recent issue, were the stockmen's and cowboys' bibles. They read the seemingly meaningless hieroglyphics with the attention of scholars and, trained as they were, could trace from them the history of the cattle industry, range by range, county by county, state by state. Early and local brand books—such as the *La Junta Tribune Brand Book* of 1886 which listed brands in Las Animas and parts of Pueblo, Huerfano, and Bent Counties in Colorado, and Colfax County in New Mexico—were usually published with descriptive cuts, two to a page, similar to the one heading this chapter, and accompanied by a large, fold-in map of the region upon which were superimposed the brands, indicating the range area of the owner's cattle. The more recent brand books, however, have dispensed with maps and engravings, and picture the brands only in small and crude line drawings, listing them, with the addresses of their owners, in double columns, forty-six brands to a single page. The books are durably bound either in leather or heavy board, printed on thin Bible paper and is- sued in narrow, notebook format, consciously in- tended for the working use of cattlemen.

The problem of locating a particular brand out of thousands—in order to determine the owner and the range—seems at first glance insurmount- able to the uninitiated. Actually, it is relatively simple, and the cowboy who uses a brand book can turn to the proper page as easily as a college stu- dent to a given word in his dictionary. All brands beginning with a letter are arranged alphabetic- ally, so that anyone looking for the A Lazy Y brand or A Quarter Circle will find it under the letter A in an ordered sequence. The same holds true for all brands beginning with a numeral, and the Two Bar X or Three Slash L are located under the nu- merals 2 and 3. Following the letters and numerals, the commonest characters with which brands be- gin are listed in sequence, normally in the order given for the *Wyoming Brand Book:* Bar, Slash, Quarter Circle, Cross, Heart, Diamond, Box, Half- Box, and Triangle. After these characters come the miscellaneous characters which are also alphabet- ized as much as possible, the Anchor brand preced- ing the Anvil and the Lazy *Ladder* following the Pocket *Knife.*

Since there are no readings for the brands, however, but only the characters themselves, a knowledge of range custom and parlance is necessary to interpret the brand orally or in written form.

Brands are read from left to right, from top to bottom, and from the outside inside:

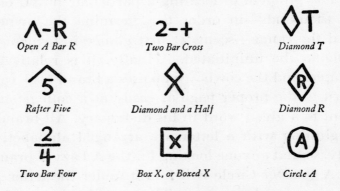

Open A Bar R	Two Bar Cross	Diamond *T*
Rafter Five	Diamond and a Half	Diamond R
Two Bar Four	Box X, or Boxed X	Circle A

An understanding of the variations possible upon a single letter was next needed in order fully to interpret a given brand. This can also best be illustrated graphically, using the letter R:

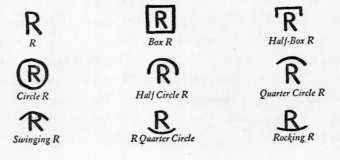

R	Box R	Half-Box R
Circle R	Half Circle R	Quarter Circle R
Swinging R	R Quarter Circle	Rocking R

Half Diamond R

Rafter R

Bar R

Bar R

R Bar

R Bar

R Bar S

R Bar S Connected

Cross R

Barbed R

R Slash

R Bench

Flying R

Walking R

Running R

Drag R

Tumbling R

Lazy R

Reverse R

Inverted R, or Crazy R

With the addition of other letters, figures, and characters, the possible combinations are almost limitless. With these, the rancher of the West— using his fertile imagination and a hot iron— turned the hides of his cattle into walking statements reflecting his humor and romance, his belief in private property and his individualism. The so-called heraldry of the range, handed down in practice from the Old World and Mexico, came into being on the Western plains.

Many ranchers were content simply to brand

their initials or, where their names were short, to burn them fully on the hide. Charles S. Wilson of Meeteetse, in Park County, Wyoming, adopted the C S W brand, and Orville A. Sturgis of Glendo used a slight variant of his initials with the O Open A S, **O∧S** . W. B. Coy of Torrington used his full name, C O Y, varying it also with C O Lazy Y and Reverse C O Lazy Y, **ɔO˂**. A. J. Olsen of Shoshoni branded his nickname, O L E, upon his stock. Lum Richards of Hope, New Mexico, registered the L U M brand; Mrs. Lura Yates of White Oaks also used her first name, L U R A; while L. W. Neatherlin of Roswell adopted the last syllable of his name, L I N.

Where men had names which lent themselves to graphic presentation, the branded characters acquired a touch of humor and a double reading, being interpreted either in terms of the symbols or, more likely, as the cattleman's real name. F. S. Harter of Wheatland, Wyoming, adopted the Heart R brand, **♡R**, and Joseph Hartle of Fort Bridger the Heart L (Inverted Heart L Connected),

♡ . B. J. Keys of Worland took the Key S, **ʃS** , the Barkey brothers of Buffalo the Bar Key, **–ʃ** , and C. D. Bell of Rimrock, Arizona, the obvious Bell, **♤** .

Unabashed proclamations of love for wife or sweetheart wandered the range, four-legged, peripatetic Valentines. Where a woman's name was short, the rancher branded it in full: L I Z, L I L, A N N, F A Y, and R A E. (All brands were commonly read by the individual letters, and "Liz" would not be LIZ but the separate L I Z. The three-letter reading would certainly be given it off the home range; locally, however, where the reason for the brand would be known, it might very well be called by the name.) Where a woman's name was too long to make an easy brand, ranchers used the Heart, which often encircled the single initial of her first name or more boldly preceded both initials. The Hearts were frequently pierced with arrows, and in the West, as elsewhere, there were Broken and Bleeding Hearts.

Men who had a penchant for gambling or were simply amused with the combination of symbols created the Seven UP brand which is found in every State, ⅂𝖴𝖯, and the KENO brand which varied from Frank Stout's in Sheridan, Wyoming, ⟋‾‾ₙₒ, to Joe Kincaid's in La Veta, Colorado, ♭ₙₒ. The aces of diamonds, clubs, and hearts were popular, but the ace of spades, interestingly enough, is conspicuous by its absence. The lucky Seven Eleven brand, 7|| , appears frequently, as do other numbers borrowed from the game of "craps" and burned on the hides in boxed dice brands.

Brands were employed as direct warnings to rustlers—PRIVATE PROPERTY, KEEP OFF!—and the readings of I C U and I Bar U at Sundance, Wyoming, were typical, as was also the 2 Bar U, $\frac{2}{U}$, of Arch Davenport at Gillette in the same state.

In New Mexico, the Navajo swastika was quickly adopted, and the English pound symbol vied with the dollar mark and identified the source of investment or hoped-for gain. The lucky and symbolic Acorn brand was widely popular, and the Cross of Christ was chosen as a mark of protection for cattle, particularly in the Southwest. Brands representing ranch equipment were burned on the stock—ladders, wrenches, mill irons, pitchforks, boots, bridle bits, houses, rakes, and knives. The moon and stars, the rising sun, mice, scissors, shoes, spoons, stockings, pants, hats, sombreros, mittens, and mirrors—whatever happened to appeal to the owner at the moment he selected his brand became his sign of possession and was registered on the hide and in the brand books. There are even brands now of locomotives, airplanes, tractors, and automobiles, reflecting the changing pace of the West, and it is not improbable that atomic symbols, Shmoos and Jeepsters have found their way into the official registers.

TYPICAL BRANDS

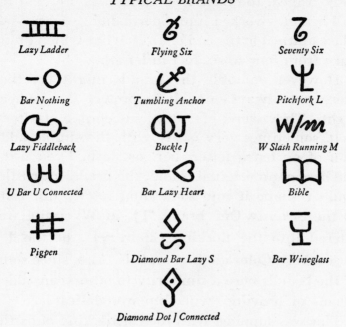

Lazy Ladder	Flying Six	Seventy Six
Bar Nothing	Tumbling Anchor	Pitchfork L
Lazy Fiddleback	Buckle J	W Slash Running M
U Bar U Connected	Bar Lazy Heart	Bible
Pigpen	Diamond Bar Lazy S	Bar Wineglass
	Diamond Dot J Connected	

The brands themselves were, in the early days, burnt on the hide with a running iron—a short bar about the length of a poker—and the cowboy simply drew or wrote the brand in a large, free-hand style, much as one might write on a blackboard. But since the running iron was an easy tool for the rustler and cattle thief to use, the carrying of it was banned by the various stock associations. A cowboy riding the range with one might be as innocent as the day was long, but on the other hand equally guilty of rustling intent. Once it was discouraged, the fixed iron came into use, and the full brand—worked into a permanent stamp—was blacksmithed to the end of an iron bar which might vary from four to six feet in length.

However valuable the brands might be, they were not always enough to protect the owner's rights. They were, of course, susceptible of alteration, sometimes very easily with the simple addition of an extra letter, bar, or slash. Even using the base of an original brand, the proficient rustler could reshape it into something totally different, as the Seventy One brand, 7I, in Wyoming was altered into the Rocking Chair, ⊤I̠ , or the J J in southern Colorado into an O U. Also, since some of the brands bore a similarity to others, an added means of proving ownership was desirable.

This was supplied with the earmarking of cattle, useful not only to help determine property rights but also for rapid identification of the animals when cutting out from the herd at the spring roundup. The special terminology of the range for these marks—

EARMARKS

Overslope

Overbit

Underslope

Underbit

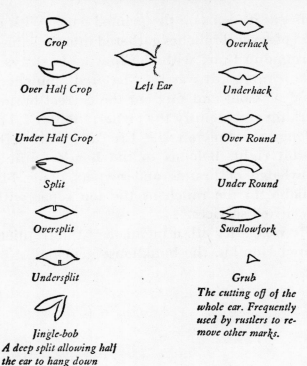

Crop

Over Half Crop

Under Half Crop

Split

Oversplit

Undersplit

Jingle-bob
A deep split allowing half the ear to hang down

Left Ear

Overhack

Underhack

Over Round

Under Round

Swallowfork

Grub
The cutting off of the whole ear. Frequently used by rustlers to remove other marks.

"crop right and swallowfork and underhack left," "overslope and underbit right and under half crop left"—was again so much unintelligible jargon to the tenderfoot. Yet the earmarks were quite as important as the brands, and were registered with them. Like the brands, they could be grouped into many different combinations.

Cowboys prided themselves on their ability to read brands and earmarks quickly, not as simple an attainment on the open range, with moving cattle, as it seems on the printed page. With many head of several ranches gathered into the same herd at roundup time, with the inevitable strays from distant ranges, it was the "lettered" puncher who could pick out and sing out the correct brand and marking and identify the owner: "Rafter L Lazy J. Belongs to Jones on Hat Creek." "Crop left and overbit right. Belongs to the Bar Z outfit." His knowledge of brands and owners made him as valuable to the ranch as the top roper with his specialized services.

He was, after all, a member of the frontier College of Heralds, the bunkhouse genealogist of the West.

THE COWBOY—like the plantation worker of the South and the sailor relaxed in the forecastle—had time on his hands for the making and remaking of songs.

The majority of these songs are not wholly indigenous to the West, but their remote origins have been sufficiently forgotten so that now most Americans think of them as "pure cowboy," unadulterated by any Eastern or European connections.

Actually, such "pure" songs as "The Streets of Laredo," "Bury Me Not on the Lone Prairie," and "The Buffalo Skinners" have clearly traceable antecedents. Where, for example, has anyone in the Southwest observed a cowboy funeral with these trappings—

> Play the fifes lowly and beat the drums slowly,
> And play the dead march as you carry me along.

The funeral was obviously a military one. And the song has been traced to an English ballad, "The Unfortunate Lad," which, in turn, may go back to an Irish song sung in Cork in the 1790's. In the English ballad, the central figure is a soldier whose comrades find him "down by Lock Hospital . . . wrapp'd in flannel, so hard is his fate," the hospital in question being a special one for social diseases, located in Harrow Road, London. The soldier of the ballad described his condition adequately:

> Had she but told me when she disordered me,
> Had she but told me of it in time,
> I might have got salts and pills of white mercury,
> But now I'm cut down in the height of my prime.

He then gave instructions for his funeral:

> Muffle your drums, play your pipes merrily,
> Play the dead march as you go along,
> And fire your guns right over my coffin,
> There goes an unfortunate lad to his home.

In the American song, the soldier has become a cowboy who has taken to drinking and gambling, and is finally shot, the lingering death from a wanton's VD replaced, in keeping with the Western scene, by the more dramatic cards and six-shooter. But the anachronistic drums and pipes, or fifes, and dead march have been retained.

Similarly, "The Ocean Burial," published in the East in 1850, was later revamped into a cow-country ballad, and a comparison of two stanzas shows the unquestioned relationship:

Oh, bury me not in the deep, deep sea,
Where the billowy shroud will roll over me,
Where no light will break through the dark, cold wave,
And no sunbeam rest upon my grave.
It matters not, I have oft been told,
Where the body shall lie when the heart is cold,
Yet grant ye, oh, grant ye, this boon to me,
Oh, bury me not in the deep, deep sea.

Oh, bury me not on the lone prairie,
Where the wild coyotes will howl o'er me,
Where the West wind sweeps and the grasses wave,
And sunbeams rest on the prairie grave.
It matters not, I've oft been told,
Where the body lies when the heart grows cold,
Yet grant, oh, grant this wish to me,
Oh, bury me not on the lone prairie.

In its passage from the East to the West, the text has been somewhat improved; it flows more easily and naturally. And the music of the Western song is a great improvement over the original. Such evolution is what folklore scholars—men like Phillips Barry and Robert W. Gordon—have called "re-creation." Not originally created by the folk, a song may, nevertheless, pass into the folk tradition through re-creation, the reworking and reshaping of the song as it is orally transmitted by many people over a considerable period of time. The difference between songs which have received such treatment and the pseudo, currently concocted ones which have not, deserves to be more widely recognized; as does also the sharp distinction between a "folksinger" and "singer of folk songs," the authentic article from the hills and the popularizer of the night clubs.

Whatever their sources, however, indigenous or borrowed, originally shaped by many hands or created by a single individual, the songs of the cowboy which may in any way be termed traditional reflect the life, language, manners, and sentiment of the West.

The most perfect gem of Western song, lyrically and musically, is "The Colorado Trail," a song which all Coloradoans should know and which the perspicacious do. Gentle and poignant, the words are sung by a cowboy presumably riding the long Colorado Trail as a restrained, Western lament for his lost or absent love:

> Eyes like the morning star,
> Cheek like a rose,

Laura was a pretty girl,
God Almighty knows.

Weep, all ye little rains,
Wail, winds, wail,
All along, along, along
The Colorado Trail.

The lyric bears favorable poetic comparison with that other anonymous gem of 16th-century England:

Oh, Western wind, when wilt thou blow
That the small rain down can rain?
Christ, that my love were in my arms
And I in my bed again.

"The Colorado Trail" is not typical. We should be rich as Croesus if it were. It is a unique and priceless bit of folk literature, folk music, and Americana. And medals should be struck by the State of Colorado for Carl Sandburg—who prints it, with the music, in his *American Songbag*—and for all others who had a hand in its preservation, including the "hoss trompled" cowboy and the doctor who first heard the cowboy singing it from his hospital cot.

More in keeping with the creak and smell of saddle leather is "The Chisholm Trail." The trail itself extended from the Washita in the Indian Territory of Oklahoma north toward Abilene and was not in Texas, even for a mile, but joined with the long Eastern Trail of that state at the Oklahoma boundary. Popularly, but incorrectly, the whole trail, from South Texas to Kansas, has been considered the Chisholm, just as there has been confusion also between Jesse Chisholm, for whom the trail was named, and John Chisum, who owned an empire with 100,000 head of cattle in New Mexico. Jesse Chisholm was a breed trapper who probably never owned a single beef but who blazed the trail southward from Kansas when he moved a body of Indians to the Territory at the Government's request.

Originating perhaps on the Chisholm Trail, although there is no certainty of this, the song spread over the whole cattle country of the West and was sung on the Western Trail into Dodge City, the Goodnight-Loving Trail into Colorado, the Stinson Trail into New Mexico, and the lesser-known trails threading hundreds of miles into the northland of Montana, Wyoming, and Idaho.

Millions of head of cattle moved over the trails, north, steadily north, to railheads and greener pastures, to the Indian Agencies and mountain ranches. The trail herds were on the move from spring to fall, long months from April to September, long miles from New Mexico to Montana. In dust and heat and storm. And the cowboy had time to make his own stanzas to "The Chisholm Trail," and to sing them to amuse himself during the slow hours of the day, or to keep the cattle quiet at night on the bed ground.

"The Chisholm Trail" is the great, single folk-song—and pure folksong—of the cowboy. It has the roll and swing of saddle and horse. It is endless, and no one ever has or ever will collect its thousands of verses. Each stanza is independent, and there is no scheme or rhyme—other than the couplets—or story to follow. Into it the cowboy, like a *cosi* making stew, threw everything at hand:

> Oh, I ride with my slicker and I ride all day,
> And I packed along a bottle for to pass the time away;
> With my feet in the stirrups and my hand on the horn,
> I'm the best damned cowboy that ever was born.
>
> Oh, I know a girl who's a-going to leave her mother,
> All the devils down in Hell couldn't stir up such another;
> She rides on a pinto and she works on the drag,
> With her petticoats a-flopping like a pair of saddlebags!
>
> Oh, I'm out night herding on the Lone Squaw Butte,
> When I run my sights on a lone coyote;
> He's a-helling and a-yelling and as he drifts by,
> I snakes out my lasso and I loops him on the fly.
>
> Oh, the shorthorns rattle and the longhorns battle,
> Never had such a ride around the locoed cattle;
> I'll trade my outfit as soon as I can,
> And I won't punch cows for no damned man.
>
> It's along 'fore daylight, they start in to feed,
> The steers all a-dragging, with the pointers in the lead;
> They head on north where the grass grows green,
> And now for the biscuits and the bacon and the beans.

No chaps, no slicker, and she pours down rain,
And I swears to my hoss I'll never ride night herd again;
Oh, I'll head back south and I'll marry me a squaw,
And live all my life on the sandy Washitaw.

Oh, I jumped on my bronco, I raked him down the flank,
Oh, he started into pitching and I landed on the bank;
Well, I leaps to my saddle and I gives a little yell,
Oh, the leaders broke the country and the cattle went
   to hell.

Oh, Abilene city is a dang fine town,
We'll liquor up and twirl those heifers all around;
Then back once more with my bridle and my hoss,
For old John Chisum is a damned fine boss.

I never hankered for to plow or hoe,
And punching steers is all I know;
With my knees in the saddle and a-hanging to the sky,
Herding dogies up in heaven in the sweet by and by.

"Git Along, Little Dogies," like "The Chisholm Trail," is a song of trail herding, but differs in that the stanzas give a descriptive and fairly connected account of the problems and purpose of driving the animals north. Of the song, Dick Devall, an old-time cowboy singer, explained: "For the benefit of all those that don't know what the word 'dogie' means, I'm going to try to tell you. A dogie is just a little calf that his mammy died in a bog hole and his daddy ran away with another cow."

As I was a-walking one morning for pleasure,
I saw a cowpuncher a-riding along,

His hat was throwed back and his spurs was a-jingling,
And as he approached he was singing this song.

Whoopee, ti-yi-oh, git along, little dogies,
It's your misfortune and none of my own,
Whoopee, ti-yi-oh, git along, little dogies,
For you know that Wyoming will be your new home.

Oh, early in the springtime we round up the dogies,
Mark 'em and brand 'em and bob off their tails,
Then round up the horses and load the chuck wagon,
And then throw the dogies out on the long trail.

Oh, some boys goes up the trail for pleasure,
But that's where they gets it most awfully wrong,
'Cause you've got no idea the trouble they give us
While we go a-driving them all along.

Oh, your mothers was raised away down in Texas,
Where the jimpson weed and the sandburrs grow,
Now we'll fill you up on prickly pear and cholla,
Till you're ready for the trail to Idaho.

Oh, you will be soup for Uncle Sam's Injuns,
It's "Beef—heap beef!" I hear them cry;
Git along, git along, git along, little dogies,
You'll be beef steers by and by.

The night herding of cattle on the trail was the
least desired assignment of the cowboy. At best—
with clear weather and quiet cattle—it was unbroken monotony, a wearisome, hours-long patrol
of the herd, doubly wearisome after the ride and
work of the day. At the worst, it was a night hell,

with driving rain and lightning, restless, fearful
beasts and the dreaded, disastrous stampede. To
control them, the cowboys talked to the cattle and
their horses, the familiar voices calming the animals. They talked to them humorously and pro-
fanely. And the part played by the strong, endless,
rolling periods of Western profanity in delivering
the beef should never be underestimated.

But in addition to rough jokes and generous
curses, the cowboys sang songs like "The Chisholm
Trail," upon which they could improvise indefi-
nitely, and still others which, because of their lazy
tempo, were identified as peculiar to night herding,
particularly for the slow nights when everything
seemed to go well. One of the best of these was "I
Ride an Old Paint" or "Ride Around, Little Dogies,"
a curious admixture of personal reflection coupled
with a bald, matter-of-fact statement about Old
Bill Jones and his very active family:

> I ride an old Paint and I lead an old Dan,
> I'm going to Montan' for to throw the hoolihan.
> They feed in the coolies, they water in the draw,
> Tails are all matted, their backs are all raw.
>
> Ride around, little dogies, ride around them slow,
> The fiery and the snuffy are a-raring to go.
>
> I've worked in the town and I've worked on the farm,
> And all I got to show is just this muscle in my arm,
> Got a blister on my foot, got a callous on my hand,
> But I'll be a cowpuncher as long as I can.

Old Bill Jones had two daughters, two daughters and a
 song,
One went to Denver and the other went wrong,
His wife she died in a poolroom fight,
Bill Jones keeps singing from morning till night.

Oh, when I die, take my saddle from the wall,
Put it on my pony, lead him out of his stall,
Tie my bones to his back, turn our faces to the West,
And we'll ride the prairie that we love the best.

Ride around, little dogies, ride around them slow,
The fiery and the snuffy are a-raring to go.

Another song which could be sung ad infinitum,
since the change of a single line was all that was
needed to vary the stanzas, was "Goodbye, Old
Paint." It was the cowboy's farewell to the bright
lights of Cheyenne before taking the long trail back
to the ranges of Montana, and the saddle roll of the
tune made it a good night herding and trail song
as well:

Goodbye, Old Paint, I'm a-leaving Cheyenne,
Goodbye, Old Paint, I'm a-leaving Cheyenne,
I'm a-leaving Cheyenne, I'm off for Montan',
Goodbye, Old Paint, I'm a-leaving Cheyenne.

Goodbye, Old Paint, I'm a-leaving Cheyenne,
Goodbye, Old Paint, I'm a-leaving Cheyenne,
My foot's in the stirrup and the rein's in my hand,
Goodbye, Old Paint, I'm a-leaving Cheyenne.

The cowboys had scores of other songs and in
Montana they had, until he was recently killed in

an automobile accident in Arizona, a great expo-
nent of them, Powder River Jack Lee. After his
range days, Powder River toured the West with his
wife, Kitty, singing on more street corners, at more
rodeos, and in more theaters, honky-tonks, schools,
and colleges than half a dozen other singers rolled
together. He was big, raw-boned, white-haired,
with a voice like an old bull and a phenomenal
memory for the songs, plus a flair for showmanship
which did not, however, detract from the authen-
ticity of his material. He knew the brief songs and
the longer ballads: "Zebra Dun," for which he
claimed Montana's Con Price as the original, bronc-
busting hero about whom the song grew; "Utah
Carroll," the story of a Utah puncher who, to save
another life, died under the hoofs of stampeding
cattle; "Preacher Dunn, the Outlaw," a wild and
unbroken bronc carrying the O Four Bar brand
from Ranchester, Wyoming, finally killed when it
turned a "sunfishing somersault" at Miles City,
Montana; the lively "Santa Fe Trail," actually
written, words and music, by a Denverite professor
of law at Yale, but passed orally and with textual
changes to Powder River; "Billy Venero," the ballad of an Apache attack in Arizona and of the cowboy who, shot and dying, tied himself to his saddle
to bring the warning news to his sweetheart at an
isolated ranch; the misanthropic "I've Got No Use
for the Women;" and "The Wyoming Nester," the

cowboys' farewell to the open range and philosophical acceptance of defeat before the advancing and hated fence builders.

But above all, Powder River, who was a Montana man to the core, delighted to let loose with Montana's war cry. His boots cocked on a table in the Windsor Hotel bar in Denver, his sombrero tipped back, a glass of whisky before him, and the guitar in his lap, he sang:

Powder River, let 'er buck, a surging mass of cattle,
Roundup wagons full of chuck, horns and hoofs a-rattle,
Steers and dogies, beefs and broncs, heaving flanks
    a-quiver,
Hear the wranglers yip, "Whoopee! Hooray for Powder
    River!"

Herders left and herders right, broncs and cutting horses,
Sougans under starry skies and wagons for the bosses,
Old chinook a-changing west, angry bulls a-booming,
Stark above the feeding grounds the Rocky Mountains
    looming.

Thundering hoofs across the range, sunburned hides and
    faces,
Twisters spinning east and west, and cowboys running
    races,
Scratch your bronc, you riding fool, a big whoopee they
    give 'er,
"We're wild and woolly, full of fleas, and bound for
    Powder River!"

Powder River wound up with a screaming "YEE-OU-H-H-H! She's one mile wide and one inch deep!

And she rolls uphill from Texas! She's a swimming hole for grasshoppers, and full of dust and flatfish! Powder River! Let 'er buck!"

Like many another folksinger, Powder River altered and changed songs, and created the new out of the old. Using this same song as a base upon which to build, Powder River honored the West's Ninety-First Division and their bloody battles at the Meuse, the Argonne, Ypres, Flanders, and St. Mihiel during the First World War. The uninhibited cowboy tradition of the West moved overseas with the Expeditionary Force, men bred in the great legacy of freedom and on a land without barriers. . . .

Powder River, let 'er buck—the foe began to shiver
When the cry swept o'er the front, "Hurrah for Powder
  River!"
Thirty thousand buckaroos on Flanders fields so bloody,
Side by side they crept and died, and each one for his
  buddy.

Shrapnel burst—the Ninety-First, with all that hell to
  blind 'em,
Thundered through the Argonne till they left the flags
  behind 'em;
Where the golden poppies grow, and glorious they quiver,
Each one represents a soul who hailed from Powder
  River.

When we landed in New York, they crowded all around
  us,

Everybody seemed to wonder where and how they found
us;
From the mountains and the plains and from the hills
and valleys,
Thirty thousand heroes left their ranches and their
Sallys.

Oh, they come through Belgium, a-whooping and
a-howling,
We're from the wild and woolly West, that's where we
do our prowling;
Everywhere the Allies stare and hand out their decision,
There's the cowboy regiments—the Ninety-First
Division.

Hear 'em yell as wild as hell, with victory to vision,
Powder River, here we come, the Ninety-First Division;
Let 'er buck, we're full of luck, we're woolly, wild, and
airy,
She's one mile wide and one inch deep from Hell to
Tipperary.

We're full of fleas from overseas and none of 'em can
match us,
Up in France we made 'em dance, it took all hell to
catch us;
When we get riled our teeth are filed, we're "pisen" to
the liver,
It's hell or burst, we're the Ninety-First—the boys from
Powder River!

THE SONGS of the cowboy have traveled to
the ends of the earth. There is a universality about
many of them—love, death, the space of the land
and sky; and the romance of the way of life on the
open range is inherent in all of them. But the songs
of the mining men of the West, the mucker and
hardrock driller, are scarcely known outside the
immediate vicinity of the mining camps themselves, and even there have received scant atten-

tion. This can be accounted for, however, in various and reasonable ways.

In the first place, the mining songs have tended to be technical in content, referring casually to the slang and jargon of the industry, to the "buzzies," "stopers," to "taking five," to "missed holes," and to "rounding in and rounding out." There is nothing technical about a man, a horse, a cow, and a prairie, or their relationship to each other in the cattle industry, nothing which cannot be understood readily from the songs. But to appreciate fully the mining songs without knowledge of the above-ground and underground workings of a mine can be done only by supplying some glossary or explanation for the majority of them. Their audience, therefore, is largely limited to the appreciative miner.

Secondly, the songs of the cowboy traveled with him as he ambled alone from one ranch to another or as he covered the long trails in company with other punchers. They were disseminated through the whole West and reached everyone. The miners' songs, on the other hand, tended to be localized as well as technical. It is true that the "boomer," or tramp miner, carried them from Butte to Jerome and from Cripple Creek to the Coeur d'Alene, and that they traveled to this extent, but they were still not disseminated throughout the region but only to the mining camps themselves. They were, therefore, more inbred than the cowboy songs.

Lastly, the music of the mining songs does not compare with that of the cowboy songs. And there is good reason for this as well. The miner, at his work, had little or no time for reflective creation. The heavy work of the mines, the sound of pick and shovel, the drilling and blasting gave him no opportunity for the making of music. And when he left the mine, he went to the local saloons to be entertained, not to entertain himself. As a result, the music of the mining songs is either distinctly inferior or, where it is not, has been borrowed *in toto* from popular songs of the day and lacks special interest because it lacks originality. This full borrowing of music—without re-creation—has been historically true of mining songs from the days of '49, when men set their own words to "Oh, Susannah" and "Massa's in the Cold, Cold Ground," to the present, when other miners currently parody "Casey Jones" and "Roaming in the Gloaming."

An exception on the musical side may be made for the Cornishmen. They were the Cousin Jacks of the West, men who fiercely prided themselves on their mining ability: "One Cornishman is worth ten other miners," "A Cousin Jack can smell ore." They brought with them to the hardrock mines of Michigan and California a centuries-old tradition of mining and an equally long tradition of music. From these states, they gravitated naturally to

Colorado, Utah, Arizona, and Nevada, wherever their experience and knowledge were in demand. And out of their pride, both for their work and musical ability, they created the "Cousin Jack Song" with its lyric which is not cheap boasting, but a clear statement of acknowledged prowess—"We Cousin Jacks can do it":

> You'll find them on the mountain tops,
> You'll find them on the plains,
> You'll find those boys where'er you go,
> And you'll find their mining claims.
>
> And for singing and for mining
> They have somehow got the knack,
> It's a second nature to that class
> Of lads called Cousin Jacks.
>
> They come from distant Tombstone
> And Virginia on the Hill,
> You ne'er can beat a Cousin Jack
> For hammering on the drill.
>
> Amongst you other Irishmen
> Do justice if you can,
> For there's none that can compete
> With the good old Cornishman.
>
> And for singing and for mining
> They have somehow got the knack,
> It's a second nature to that class
> Of lads called Cousin Jacks.

The miner of the early, bustling camps—like the cowboy with his range to ride—preferred his way

of life to any other. And as idealized as "Home on
the Range," to which it bears a stanzaic relation
although the tune is dissimilar, was a song giving
an account of life in one of the high mining camps
of the Rocky Mountains. R. C. Warner of Denver
sang it and he, in turn, had heard it sung at Idaho
Springs by Springheel Riley, "the wildest little
agitatin' Irishman you ever knew." It is sufficiently
old to have retained in it the former name of the
Colorado River, the Grand, still used by old-timers.

Oh, give me the hills and the ring of the drills
And the rich silver ore in the ground,
Where seldom is heard a discouraging word
And many true friends will be found.

Oh, give me the camp where the prospectors tramp
And business is always alive,
Where dance halls come first and the faro banks burst,
And every saloon is a dive.

Oh, give me the steed and the gun that I need,
Shoot game from my own cabin door,
With Glenwood below where the one-lungers go,
And we'll camp on the banks of the Grand.

Oh, give me the wife, the pride of my life,
She can ride, she can shoot like a man,
She's a fond and true heart, and we never will part,
Together we'll roam through the land.

Oh, give me the hills and the roaring stamp mills,
And the riches that in the hills lie,
We'll work and we'll play all the livelong day,
Oh, there let me live till I die.

Saloons, faro banks, dance halls, the roar of stamp mills, the sound of drills! Yet this was in keeping with the tenor of mining-camp life, and the spirit has been retained in later songs which continue the tradition. The songs are rough and boisterous. They state the facts of the mine, not in any sense of "protest" but in a casual, reportorial manner, a "this is the way it was, partner." They contain the pride of men for their own camps, their joshing contempt for workers from other mines, their natural cussing at the shift bosses and frequent references to whisky, women, and general off-shift uproar.

The Butte miners are particularly vocal, and even a stanza on the delights of Meaderville winds up with a belligerent Irish chip on the shoulder. A good brawl, after all, meant a successful evening:

> There's women up to Meaderville,
> The whisky it is swell,
> And if yez Bisbee men don't like it,
> Yez can all go to hell!

To the tune of "My Bonnie Lies Over the Ocean," however, the miner contemplated the ultimate effect of too many good times:

> I'm only a broken-down miner,
> You can tell by the looks of my clothes,
> I've spent all my dough on the women,
> How much Jesus Christ only knows!

The men appreciated short ditties rather than
the longer ballads:

> Down in the hole we go, boys,
> Down in the hole we go,
> The two thousand level
> Is hot as the devil—
> I envy the man with the hoe!

And from Utah, a stanza, sung to "Roaming in
the Gloaming," celebrated the pleasures of working for the Vanadium Corporation of America:

> Oh, I guzzle the very worst way,
> I work for VCA,
> Oh, I'm proud of the country
> And the place where I was born.
> Oh, I sing a jolly rhyme
> And have a merry time,
> And leave a little in the bottle
> For the morning.

And of more recent creation still and adapted to
the air of "I'm a Rambling Wreck:"

> I'm a roaring son of the Comstock
> And I work in the Chollar Mine,
> I fight my whisky with both hands
> And never have a dime;
>
> And when I'm dead and lying
> In a coffin bound for hell,
> I'll still be a son of the Comstock
> And the devil knows it well.

More realistic and descriptive of the ups and downs of the itinerant miner's life is "The Tramp Miner's Song." It was a song sung in many camps, the names of the bosses—here Eddie Kane and the King—and the mines—the Diamond, Mountain Con, and Neversweat—changed to suit the locality and the whim of the singer. The tramp miner "dragged his time" for many reasons: because he had worked enough to acquire a stake to take him elsewhere in his hunt for greener pastures; because he was a footloose tourist incapable of settling into a "home guard camp" with any family; because he worked with a chip on his shoulder and wound up on the losing end of a fight with a shift boss or fellow worker; or, simply and frequently, because he got roaring drunk and, unable to show up for his next shift, had to quit. Many tramp miners were excellent machinemen and miners, and the bosses hired them quickly, aware that they would work only a month or two; others, however, who had acquired notorious reputations as "two-day miners" and who had no training beyond the "muck stick," were as quickly rejected. Their way of life was of their own choosing—except, of course, as mines closed and everyone was affected—and the singer of the Butte version given here states his independent case clearly, closing on a realistic note of joblessness:

There were miners from Bisbee
And machinemen from Butte,
And cowboys from Polson
To muck rock down in the chute.

And I got me a job
On the first day of May,
And five-and-a-quarter,
They said that was the pay.

And I worked four shifts,
And I dragged my time,
The hell with Eddie Kane
And his big Diamond Mine!

And I went to the Coeur d'Alene
And I rustled the King,
But he said, "For a tramp like you
There isn't a thing."

So I went back to Butte
And I rustled the Con,
And I rustled the Sweat,
And the winter is over
And I'm rustling yet.

The caste distinction between the lowly mucker who shoveled the broken rock and the miner who worked the drill, referred to above in the derogatory "cowboys from Polson," is clear also in the two following ditties, both of them sung to "Turkey in the Straw":

Says the mucker to the miner,
"If I give you a chew,

Will you make me a miner
Just the same as you?"

Says the miner to the mucker,
"That would never do,
You can't be a miner
Till you can drink, swear, and chew."

And the special point of the second version depends on the fact that the wages of the mucker are less than those of the trained driller and the latter should, on all counts, be better able to supply himself with the small luxuries of mining life:

Says the miner to the mucker,
"Will you give me a chew?"
Says the mucker to the miner,
"I'm damned if I do.

"Save up your money
And save up your rocks,
And you'll always have a chew
In your old tobacco box!"

The hardrock men, who worked with steel and drill, singlejack and doublejack—the heavy hammers—and dynamite to break down the face of the mine and drive their tunnels deeper into the earth, were the recognized lords of the shift. Any man could shovel muck as long as his back held up. But the driller, working alone or with a partner, had to strike the drill with precision, turn it around with each blow so that it would not stick in the hole as a nail is driven in wood but would have loose play, and then "spoon out" the hole and tamp in the dynamite. There was a science also to the number and location of holes to be drilled in a single "round," and the men who knew the "ground" and angled the holes could break double the rock that a green driller could. The green driller was liable to hear insults from the mucker: "Hell, I can go in there with a cigar box and a tom-cat and haul more muck than you can break in a shift!" But the great drillers, like Ingersoll Slim, kept muckers and mules and ore carts moving steadily and bowed to no one. They were proud of their position in the mine and boasted of it:

> We're the hardrock men and we work underground,
> And we don't want sissies or foremen around,
> We work all day and we work all night,
> And we live on powder and DYNAMITE!
>
> Then slam it with a singlejack and turn it around!
> We're the hardrock men and we work underground!
> We work underground in the candle light,
> And we live on powder and DYNAMITE!
>
> Old Johnny Deen used lots of dynamite,
> He crimped all his caps with a single bite,
> But he got some new teeth from a dentist one day,
> And the first cap he bit blew his whole head away!
>
> Then pull out the steel from the hole in the rock,
> And put in the spoon and heave out the muck!
> Fill her up with powder and tamp her down tight,
> And break down the face with DYNAMITE!

Oh, sometimes she shoots when you don't want her to,
And then she won't shoot spite of all that you do,
And that's why dynamite is just like a mule,
And the man who says it ain't, he's a goldarned fool!

Then slam it with a singlejack and turn it around!
We're the hardrock men and we work underground!
We work underground by the candle light,
And we live on powder and DYNAMITE!

There are few songs of tragedy and death in the mines, and those few which do exist seem to have come to the West with miners who brought them from the Joplin area or from the East. Working close to death, the Western miner chose to ignore it or to treat it humorously in his songs. Just as old Johnny Deen passed on suddenly, so also did Casey Jones, metamorphosed into a "ten day" miner working behind a modern drilling machine. When a charge of dynamite "won't shoot spite of all that you do," it is termed a "missed hole." Miners, blasting the face, carefully count each charge of the round as it detonates, and, where a hole misses, cautiously wait before returning to inspect their work, allowing ample time for a slow-burning or faulty fuse to explode the charge. But even with all due caution, miners are occasionally trapped at the critical moment, killed by flying rock and the force of the delayed blast. This was the fate which met Casey, returning to work after "taking five" minutes of loafing time on the job.

Come all you muckers and gather here,
A story I'll tell you of a miner dear,
Casey Jones was the miner's name,
On a Burleigh machine he won his fame.

> Casey Jones was a ten day miner,
> Casey Jones was a ten day man,
> Casey Jones took a chance too many,
> And now he's mining in the Promised Land.

The story I am about to tell
Happened at a mine called the Liberty Bell;
They went into the crosscut and mucked her out,
And Casey said, "We'd better step about."

Casey said, "We'd better dig in
Before that damned old shift boss comes in;
If he finds out we've been taking five,
He'll send us to the office to get our time."

They went into the crosscut, put up the bar,
Placed the machine up on the arm,
Put in a starting drill with its bit toward the ground,
Turned on the air and she began to pound.

Casey said, "If I haven't lied,
There is a missed hole on that right-hand side."
His partner said, "Oh, gracious me,*
If it ever went off where would we be!"

They went into the crosscut to drill some more,
The powder exploded with a hell of a roar,
It scorched poor Casey just as flat as a pan,
And now he's a-mining in the Promised Land.

---

* Determined by the exigencies of the rhyme, these words are probably the most unlikely ever recorded in the whole history of the mining West!

Casey said just before he died,
"There's one more machine I would like to have tried."
His partner said, "What can it be?"
"An Ingersoll jackhammer, now don't you see."

Casey Jones was a ten day miner,
Casey Jones was a ten day man,
Casey Jones took a chance too many,
And now he's mining in the Promised Land.

T HE MORMONS built on the land soundly
and greatly in the face of contumely, prejudice,
and the obstacles of nature. They were pioneers of
the West who were hard-working, persevering, and
realistic. They were humble and selfless, accepting
their assigned communal duties; and they were
proud and arrogant men with faith and vision.

Much has been written of them, much which
was derogatory and shameful, much which has

been regretted. But with the healing of wounds and the passage of time, with the perspective of history and the sloughing away of the ephemerally sensational, their real greatness and contribution to the West has been recognized. And their accomplishments, together with the spirit which motivated them, can be found in songs of their own making, traditional songs which have only recently been systematically collected and gathered together.

Harried and harassed as the Mormons were in Missouri and Illinois by "mobocracy," they emigrated West in 1848 to establish their headquarters at Salt Lake, the site chosen by Brigham Young and determined on the spot by his now famous words, "This is the place." With the Gold Rush emigrations of the following year a certain prosperity came to the "city" as an outfitting and trading post, but its permanent place was assured with the introduction of large-scale irrigation—the first practiced in the United States—and with the arrival of added converts to the Mormon cause who came as permanent settlers from the East and from Europe.

Poor as many of these emigrants were, they lacked the wherewithal to equip themselves properly for the long journey across the plains and mountains. There was no money for the heavy wagons or for horses and oxen. Undaunted, however, they undertook the most fantastic mass mi-

gration in the history of our country. From the
Missouri Valley to Salt Lake, a distance of a thousand miles, they walked, pushing high-wheeled
handcarts containing their few possessions and the
smallest of the children. Between 1856 and 1861,
more than four thousand emigrants made the journey in this fashion, a journey which was difficult
for all and disastrous to scores who perished on the
road. "The Handcart Song," to encourage emigra-
tion and to cheer the travelers on the journey, was
created:

> Ye saints who dwell on Europe's shore,
> Prepare yourselves forever more
> To leave behind your native land,
> For sure God's judgments are at hand;
> For you must cross the raging main
> Before the promised land you gain,
> And with the faithful make a start
> To cross the plains with your handcart.
>
> For some must push and some must pull
> As we go marching up the hill,
> So merrily on our way we go
> Until we reach the valley-oh.
>
> The lands that boast of modern light
> We know are all as dark as night,
> Where poor men toil and want for bread,
> Where peasant hosts are blindly led;
> These lands that boast of liberty
> You ne'er again would wish to see,
> When you from Europe make a start
> To cross the plains with your handcart.

As on the road the carts are pulled,
'Twould very much surprise the world
To see the old and feeble dame
Thus lend a hand to pull the same;
And maidens fair will dance and sing,
Young men more happy than the king,
And children, too, will laugh and play,
Their strength increasing day by day.

But some will say, "It is too bad,
The saints upon the foot to pad,
And, more than that, to pull a load
As they go marching o'er the road."
But then we say, "It is the plan
To gather up the best of men,
And women, too, for none but they
Will ever travel in this way."

And long before the valley's gained,
We will be met upon the plain
With music sweet and friends so dear
And fresh supplies our hearts to cheer;
And then with music and with song
How cheerfully we'll march along,
And thank the day we made a start
To cross the plains with our handcarts.

The last stanza was not mere illusory propaganda. The Mormons planned well, and as parties of emigrants toiled westward, a constant relay of mounted riders informed Salt Lake of their progress, deaths due to accident or disease, and the status of dwindling supplies. When parties were weakened or it became evident that their supplies were running dangerously low, Brigham Young ordered wagon trains east to their assistance. One such train, composed of young men from Sanpete County, trekked eastward in June, 1868, without mishap until they reached the swollen Green River. Here the main wagons were ferried across the treacherous waters, but the oxen, balking, refused to ford. Using the ferry in a final effort to get them over, the boat overturned in midstream, sweeping six men to their deaths. This rare song was composed by surviving members of the group while completing their trip to bring aid to the emigrants:

> We, the boys of Sanpete County,
> In obedience to the cause,
> Started out with forty wagons
> To bring emigrants across.
> To accomplish our great mission
> We were called to fill below,
> We left our friends and dear relations
> O'er the dreary plains to go.
>
> Over hills and by the fountains,
> Through the mud and in the dust,
> Slowly climbed the lofty mountains,
> Far above the snow's white crust.
> And we reached the Green River ferry,
> On her banks all night we stayed,
> Morning ferriéd our wagons,
> Thinking soon to roll away.
>
> Next to drive our cattle over,
> But we found they would not swim,

Though the boys were in the water
Many hours to their chins;
And the mighty winds were blowing
All the day and night before,
And the gurgling, rushing waters
Drove our cattle back to shore.

As the boys were passing over,
Water in the boat did pour;
Captain cried, "Boys, we've gone under,
We shall die this very hour!"
Down they went and crushed by tackling
'Neath those waters all went down,
And that mighty, rushing current
Swept them up with objects 'round.

Some to oxen's horns were clinging
Till with them life's step was o'er,
Boys and cattle all went under,
Ne'er again to step on shore.
These six boys from parents taken
And from friends whom they did love,
But we soon again shall meet them
In that better Land above.

Once arrived in Utah, however, the emigrants
were faced with the necessity of supporting themselves and, under the direction of Church authorities, of expanding the Deseret empire. One of the
most thankless tasks assigned any single group of
them was to establish the town of St. George in the
remote southwestern corner of the state and there
to produce cotton crops. This Dixie of Utah—so
named as a region even to this day—was barren,

dry, and a seemingly hopeless place for pioneer agriculture. No one in his right mind would have chosen to go on the mission. But the men and their families, under the rigorous discipline of the early Church, did not choose—they were chosen. Notified that they had been selected to pull up stakes and go, many of them reacted quickly with a "By God, I won't do it!" Then, after a few minutes' reflection and communion with their souls, their next remark was a changed, "All right, if we've got to go, we'd better start packing." Crops failed year after year. The "town" itself was nothing more than two rows of wagons lined up facing each other along the main "street." Women who had been accustomed to the relative luxuries of Salt Lake here had nothing. A single, desert wild flower was a rarity. Some settler, with a sense of humor in the face of hardship and who stayed with the town long enough to watch it grow, produced the song "St. George" with its four-line chorus, the first two lines frankly derisive and the last two as hopeful as any Chamber of Commerce could desire. Today the town has over 3,500 people and is a permanent fixture on the industrious Mormon landscape.

> Oh, what a dreary place this was
> When first the Mormons found it;
> They said no white man here could live,
> And Indians prowled around it.

They said the land it was no good
And the water was no gooder,
And the bare idea of living here
Was enough to make men shudder.

    Mesquite! Soap-root!
    Prickly-pears and briers!
    St. George ere long will be a place
    That everyone admires!

Now green lucerne in verdant spots
Redeems our thriving city,
Whilst vines and fruit trees grace our lots
With flowers sweet and pretty,
Where once the grass in single blades
Grew a mile apart in distance,
And kept the crickets on the hop
To pick up their subsistence.

The sun it is so scorching hot,
It makes the water sizz, sir,
And the reason that it is so hot
Is just because it is, sir.
The wind with fury here doth blow
So that when we plant or sow, sir,
We place one foot upon the seeds
And hold them till they grow, sir.

The Mormons extolled their industry, not only in other songs about their towns—"Parowan, My Parowan"—but also in two songs relating to their part in the building of the Central Pacific which joined with the Union Pacific at Promontory Point in 1869 to form the first transcontinental railroad.

Two groups of men, one in Weber or Weaver Canyon and the other in Echo Canyon, labored at the request of Brigham Young to assist in completing the railroad. Each group composed and sang a song, both of which have been preserved orally as well as in the records of the state. The Echo Canyon men were highly enthusiastic:

In the Canyon of Echo, there's a railroad begun,
And the Mormons are cutting and grading like fun,
They say they'll stick to it until it's complete,
For friends and relations are longing to meet.

Hurray! Hurrah! The railroad's begun!
Three cheers for our contractor, his name's Brigham
Young.
Hurray! Hurrah! We're light-hearted and gay,
Just the right kind of boys to build a railway.

Our camp is united, we all labor hard,
And if we are faithful, we'll gain our reward;
Our leader is wise and a great leader, too,
And all things he tells us, we're right glad to do.

The boys in our camp are light-hearted and gay,
We work on the railroad ten hours a day;
We're thinking of fine times we'll have in the fall,
When we'll be with our ladies and go to the ball.

We surely must live in a very fast age:
We've traveled by ox team and then took the stage,
But when such conveyance is all done away,
We'll travel in steam cars upon the railway.

The great locomotive next season will come
To gather the saints from their far-distant home,
And bring them to Utah in peace here to stay
While the judgments of God sweep the wicked away.

By comparison, the men in Weber Canyon, who had come from Logan, Utah, at Brigham Young's behest in 1868, were downright pessimistic. While some good might come out of the iron horse, it was going to bring Hell's own problems as well:

The iron horse draweth nigh
With its smoke-nostrils high,
Eating fire while he grazes,
Drinking water while he blazes;
And the steam forces out,
Whistles loud, "Clear the route!"
For the iron horse is coming
With a train in his wake.

We have isolated been,
But soon we shall be seen,
Through this wide mountain region
Folks can learn of our religion;
Saints will come, sinners, too,
We'll have all that we can do,
For this great Union Railroad
It will fetch the Devil through!

But the general optimism and belief in the Mormon future could scarcely be downed by a single group of skeptics. To the tune of "Marching Through Georgia," they sang jubilantly:

There's Utah and the Mormons
In Congress, pulpit, press,
Utah and the Mormons
In every place, I guess;
We must be growing greater,
We can't be growing less,
For all are talking of Utah.

Hurrah, Hurrah!
The Mormons have a name,
Hurrah! Hurrah!
They're on the road to fame;
No matter what they style us,
We're all about the same,
For all are talking of Utah.

Serious as they were about their cause and their
economic progress, the Mormons were not above
poking fun at themselves, particularly as they became assured of their position in the American
scene and no longer feared persecution. The visitor
to Salt Lake City today is certain to have called
to his attention, if he himself does not notice it,
that Brigham Young's statue is turned rearward
toward the Temple while an outstretched hand
points importantly forward toward the bank. It is
a part of current local folklore. Also, as time quiet-
ed the uproar about polygamy, the Mormons, with
latter-day humor, have sung of the trials and tribu-
lations of their many-wived forbears, not with any
disrespect—for Brother Brigham is still their great
leader—but with the same distant astonishment

accorded Solomon. The song, "Brigham, Brigham Young," however, once precipitated riots in the mining camps of Tintic and Eureka between Mormon settlers and the "Gentile" miners who created it:

Old Brigham Young was a Mormon bold,
  And a leader of the roaring rams,
And a shepherd of a heap of pretty little sheep,
  And a nice fold of pretty little lambs.
And he lived with five-and-forty wives
  In the city of Great Salt Lake,
Where they woo and coo as pretty doves do
  And cackle like ducks to a drake.

    Brigham, Brigham Young—
      'Tis a miracle he survives,
    With his roaring rams, his pretty little lambs,
      And five-and-forty wives.

Number forty-five was about sixteen,
  Number one was sixty-three,
And among such a riot how he ever keeps them quiet
  Is a downright mystery to me.
For they clatter and they claw, and they jaw, jaw, jaw,
  Each one has a different desire;
It would aid the renown of the best shop in town
  To supply them with half what they require.

Old Brigham Young was a stout man once,
  But now he is thin and old,
And I love to state, there's no hair on his pate
  Which once wore a covering of gold,
For his youngest wives won't have white wool,
  And his old ones won't take red,

So in tearing it out they have taken turn about,
   Till they've pulled all the wool from his head.

Now if anybody envies Brigham Young,
   Let them go to Great Salt Lake,
And if they have leisure to examine at their pleasure,
   They'll find it's a great mistake.
One wife at a time, so says my rhyme,
   Is enough for the proudest Don,
So e'er you strive to live lord of forty-five,
   Live happy if you can with one.

IN A LAND whose northernmost reaches are
sometimes buried under drifts of snow sixty and a
hundred feet deep, and whose southern stretches are
populated with horned toads, Gila monsters, scor-
pions, and other creatures of the desert, it was inevitable that tall tales should grow and flourish.

The makings were at hand. And, oddly enough,
the incredulity of the East about this spacious domain literally forced the creation of the tales.

Jim Bridger, trapper and mountain man extraordinary, who had discovered the Yellowstone, reported the physical characteristics of what is now the Park area to the editor of the *Kansas City Journal*, one Horn, in the 1840's. Horn, believing the sincerity of Bridger and his description of the "place where all hell bubbled up," prepared an article on the subject for his readers. Before he could publish it, however, he was subjected to ridicule by friends who characterized Bridger as at least a liar, if not mentally unsound. Horn thereupon refused to print Bridger's account. More than thirty years later, he had the good grace publicly to apologize to the trapper. But in the meantime, because people would not believe his "tales" about the Yellowstone, Bridger—who loved a good yarn in any case—resolved that the public should have just cause for doubting him. And yet even his tall tales have some Western basis in fact—the obsidian cliffs, petrified forests, boiling springs, and geysers.

Bridger told listeners of the glass mountain he had found while on a hunting trip. He had first seen, directly before him, not more than thirty yards distant, a magnificent elk calmly grazing. Taking careful aim, Bridger fired. Not only was the animal not hit, but it made no move at the sound of the gun. Bridger, much to his own astonishment, fired a second and a third time without effect. He grew so infuriated at himself, the complacent elk, and the

whole unnatural proceedings that he rushed wildly
at the animal, intending to use his gun as a club to
kill it—but suddenly crashed into an immovable,
vertical wall which, on examination, proved to be a
mountain of perfectly transparent glass. Not only
was it pure glass, but it was also a perfect telescopic
lens, and the elk which had seemed only a few yards
away was, in actuality, twenty-five miles distant.

According also to Bridger, there existed in the
Park country a mountain which was once cursed by
a great medicine man of the Crow Indian Nation.
Everything on the mountain was petrified instantly
and has remained so ever since. Sagebrush, grass,
prairie fowl, antelope, elk, and bear may be seen
there just as they once were in actual life. Even
flowers bloom eternally in natural color, birds soar
with wings spread in motionless flight, and the sun
and the moon shine with petrified light. The law of
gravity itself was petrified, and Bridger was able to
ride across a deep canyon without falling. "It was
a-all-ll pew-tree-fied, gentlemen, a-all-ll pew-tree-
fied."

Anyone who has visited the west shore of Yellowstone Lake knows how simple a matter it is to catch
the lake trout and, without removing them from the
line, to cook them in the nearby boiling pools. But
Bridger had an even better arrangement. He discovered an immense boiling spring which discharged its hot waters directly into the lake. The

specific gravity of this water, owing to the expansive action of heat, was less than that of the cool lake water, and it floated in a stratum three or four feet thick upon the cold water underneath. When Bridger was in need of fish, it was to this spot that he went. Through the hot upper stratum, he let fall his bait to the colder waters beneath and, having hooked his fish, cooked it as he pulled it out. This simplified his housekeeping problems considerably, as did also the marvelous echo which acted as an alarm clock. At night Bridger shouted, "Get up! Get up!" and in the morning, timed to his needs, the echo wakened him.

Another discovery of his was an ice-cold spring located near the summit of a high mountain, the water from which flowed down over a long, smooth slope, attaining such velocity that, as a result of friction, it was boiling hot when it reached the bottom. Bridger also had known of a prospector employing a similar smooth slope to hasten his mountain descent. The man had sat on a shovel, using it as a sled. When he failed to return to camp, however, his companions searched for him and found nothing but an infusible clay pipe and the molten remains of what had been his shovel. Hasty descents ceased to be popular.

Bridger also had the uncanny ability of estimating the elevation of any point in the West. His method of doing so was relatively easy: he simply bored a hole in the ground until he struck salt water and then dropped a line to measure the distance above sea level.

And once, taking advantage of a seventy-foot fall of snow which trapped and froze many buffaloes around Salt Lake, Bridger rolled the animals into the lake and for a long period was able to supply the Indians with pickled buffalo.

In this land where everything was big it was inevitable that all birds, beasts, and even bugs should be mammoth, and that the weather with all its phenomena should be something to talk about. In the Bridger tradition the tales flowed out of the West. Bedbugs were so large that when miners routed them out of bed, they hopped onto the bureaus and chandeliers and barked at the men. Lake fishing was difficult: "Constable Baldwin says the mosquitoes are bigoted and revengeful. You can do nothing with them. When you get after them with a brush of boughs, they get mad at not being allowed to have their own way. They then get up on the hillside and throw rocks." Settlers in Montana and Idaho thought to protect themselves from the insects by sleeping under iron kettles, but the mosquitoes drilled holes in the kettles, hooked their bills through them, and hoisted them off the quaking pioneers. Grasshoppers were big enough to drive as horses for spring plowing, and trained pet snakes were used by stage drivers to link both front and rear wheels and brake the stages going down hill.

It is so hot in Yuma that its residents are buried in overcoats to protect them when they reach Hell. When a storm sets in in Montana, the wind strips the feathers off chickens, pins cats and dogs against the barns ten feet off the ground, and snaps wagon chains. The Washoe zephyr howls over Mount Davidson, lifts tin roofs, flattens wooden shacks, stacks citizens' hats in fifteen-foot drifts down Six Mile Canyon and, on one occasion, picked up a mule which flew braying through the air from Virginia City to Dayton. "Times were very lively at Charley Legate's street oyster-stand during the late gale. About four o'clock, the poor oysters began to blow out of their shells—uttering the most piercing shrieks as they flew along and landed in the cold mud. The clams would have fared no better, but seeing how things were going, they jumped down off the stand and ran under the sidewalk for shelter, spinning along as nimbly as a flock of quail." And a Comstock wind on August 12, 1871, created considerable uproar: "The air was filled with dust, rags, paper, ejaculations, and execrations. A man called another a liar on B Street and the words were swept away to the corner of C and Union streets, where they were whirled round and round in an eddy, and a man who happened to be standing there was knocked down and had the end of his nose bitten off by his best friend, who was passing and thought the

man was wild to fight him. Many similar mistakes
occurred about town, but we have room for but one
more instance. A man on C street asked a friend to
take a drink, but that friend never heard him at all,
the words being carried away to D street where they
were caught upon a lamppost, against which two
thirsty souls (with hearts that beat as one) were
leaning. Each supposed the other had asked him to
take a drink, and the consequence was that they
followed each other about town until both got sober
in trying to get drunk."

A prospector's fierce comment to a buzzard in the
hot country of New Mexico characterized his feelings: "You damned black bird, you've got wings and
you stay here!" Places in the West were described
as being "a thousand miles from hay and grain,
seventy miles from wood, fifteen miles from water,
and only twelve inches from hell." In such country
lived Dick Wick Hall, in the town of Salome, Arizona, midway between Wickenburg and the California line. His gas station sported a sign: "Smile,
you don't have to stay here but we do." And his
mimeographed newspaper, *The Salome Sun*,
brought him local (Salome, population, one hundred) and statewide recognition as a humorist. He
bragged of the fertility of the soil: "Melons don't do
very well here because the vines grow so fast they
wear the melons out dragging them around the
ground." And he told the story of Mac, the Yale

sprinter who took a job herding sheep in Arizona several weeks before the lambing season, and was warned by Reed, his boss, not to lose any of the lambs:

"The sheep and Mac soon disappeared in the brush and nothing more was thought of them until suppertime came and no sign of Mac or the sheep. Reed commenced to worry—about the sheep—and about seven o'clock was about to start out looking for them when Mac at last came driving them up through the brush into the corral and, after shutting them in, came up to the chuck tent, streaked with dust and perspiration and, from all appearances, tired out. Before Reed could say anything Mac burst out:

" 'Boss,' he said, 'I'm through. They thought back East that I was a foot racer, but I'm not. Almost any sheepherder that can herd that band for a week and not lose those lambs can beat all the world's records. I didn't lose any today and I ran every one of those damn lambs back into the band every time they tried to get away, but one day is enough for me. I'm all in, but they are all there. Go and count them up and then give me my time. I'm done.'

"Reed, knowing that there were no lambs in the band and that none of the ewes could have lambed yet, went down to the corral to investigate and, off in one corner, huddled up by themselves, he counted 47 jackrabbits and 16 cottontails."

The loneliness of certain occupations forced men to become humorists to retain their sanity, and one such was Sergeant John T. O'Keefe, who spent three years in the 1870's on Pikes Peak recording wind velocities, rain and snowfalls, temperatures, and other phenomena for the United States Signal Corps. He reported two violent eruptions which turned the Peak into a flaming volcano. The second of these "began with a tremendous burst which shook Pikes Peak to its very foundations, hurling into the air dense clouds of ashes and lava. The explosions succeeded each other with rapidity and increased in violence for about an hour, when the volcano seemed to enter a profound sleep. No doubt Colorado Springs will meet the same fate as Pompeii and Herculaneum."

One evening, alarmed by screams, the same Sergeant O'Keefe rushed into his bedroom to find his wife besieged by an enormous number of ferocious, carnivorous pack rats. With rare presence of mind he encased her in zinc roofing material and then, to protect his legs, thrust them into two lengths of stovepipe and began to battle the rats with a heavy club. He was making very little headway against the army of rodents, who had already eaten a quarter of beef and his small daughter, when his wife, also with great presence of mind, threw a wire loop over her husband and attached it to a powerful storage battery. The heavy current electrocuted the rats nibbling at the sergeant and made it possible for him, by alternately electrocuting some and clubbing others, to rout the enemy.

Certain of these reports astonished Washington. Perhaps because of them or because of the intrepid Sergeant's battle with pack rats, he was removed to less dangerous climes.

Like Bridger, whose truth was not believed, a Nevada miner returned East to his home town and casually described a prospecting trip of two days during which he and his partner traveled with their wagon through rain, mud, dust, snow, and blistering heat. For this account he was made an honorary member of the local liar's club and disgustedly returned West, resolved never to tell the truth again. Where truth would not go down, however, the tall tale did. An old lady from California visited a Nevada town and expressed her astonishment at the rapid flight of time. "I do declare," said she, "I get up, breakfast, and have hardly time to turn around before it is noon." "It is always so here," said her host, "time passes very rapidly here. It is on account of the extreme rarity of the atmosphere, you know." "La, yes," said the old lady, "I did know that once, but had forgotten it."

Similarly, the proprietor of a Western hotel, constructed in the last century without fire escape or other special egress in the event of disaster, was asked by a visitor occupying a third-floor room what

the procedure was in case of fire. To which the
owner replied, "Jump out of the window and turn
left." This seemed to satisfy the questioner completely.

In a country where rivers go underground and
where men dig holes in the sand to fish through
them for trout, it is possible also to believe that during dust storms the unfortunate fish aboveground
have to swim with the wind—either up or down-
stream—to keep the dust out of their eyes. And
when it becomes so cold that innocent greenhorns
can unwittingly rub off their frozen ears and go
blind looking at snow, when cows freeze standing
up, one may credit the terrible cold at Como in
1880:

"Last evening, in the cold moonlight, we saw a
figure poling itself down the side of the mountain
through the snow from Como. It was an exaggerated
image of Santa Claus, as regarded fur coat-collar,
beard, and hair. It required the whole mountain
range of Como to form a background for this figure
as it descended, so wide was the expanse of fluffy
hair of head and beard, so broad was the spread of
coat tail and neck and waist wraps, and so vast the
clouds of steam that poured from its nostrils and
encircled it like a halo.

" ' Was it cold in Como?' said the figure, repeating
our question in a hollow voice.

"It then planted its two-handed staff well to the

front, and, leaning forward upon the tripod thus formed, regarded us for a space with glazed eyes— eyes out of which seemed frozen every expression save pity for our ignorance. 'Was it cold in Como?' slowly repeated the figure, and a sort of sneer gathered on its face.

"The gaze of the creature was so unwholesome that we were sorry we had provoked it. When it again solemnly said, 'Was it cold in Como?' we felt a chill, puffed out with its frosty breath, that went to the very marrow of our bones; frost gathered on our beard; our ears began to tingle and our teeth to chatter.

"This was enough. We saw how it was. All the people of Como were frozen to death and this thing —representing the ghosts of all—had come down the mountain to give the living of the land a hint of their fate.

"As we turned to flee from the spot, a crash as of ice falling shattered to the ground greeted our ears, and, turning, we saw that the figure was gone.

"Turning to a passing pedestrian we asked, 'Did you observe just now a crash as of falling, smashing, and tinkling ice?'

" 'I did,' said the man. 'It must have been a quantity of snow and icicles falling from the eaves of some roof.'

" 'What roof?' said we, glancing about.

" 'Some roof near at hand, wasn't it?' and the man looked rather uncertain.

"Turning to leave the stranger, we heard a voice say, 'Was it cold in Como?'

" 'Did you speak, sir?' said we, facing about.

" 'No, sir, but I thought you did.'

" 'Indeed; what did you think you heard?'

" 'I thought you asked: Was it cold in Como?' "

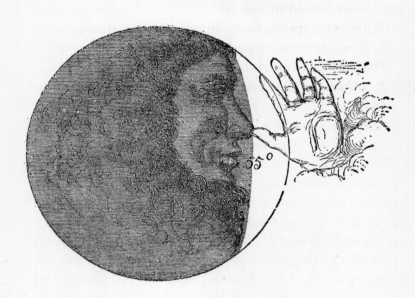

THE EARLY newspapers of the West were essentially personal in character. The owners and reporters were lords of all they surveyed and gave not one tinker's damn for the opinions of the outside world or of their rivals. They potshot at each other editorially and, in literal fact, often resorted to guns to settle their disputes. They had more fun than a barrel of monkeys and kept themselves and their subscribers wide awake. So awake, in fact, that the

editor of the *Central Utah Press* reported in 1879:
"This thing is becoming awful. Nearly every news-
paperman in the Territory during the past year has
received a terrible thrashing." There were no such
things as wire service, syndicated and synthetic
columns, or boiler plate.

Where the very names of the papers were color-
ful, the reporting was doubly so. It would be taxing
belief to imagine that the columns of the *Cripple
Creek Crusher*, the *Arizona Kicker*, the *Gringo and
Greaser*, the Ouray *Solid Muldoon*, the *Missing
Link*, and the *Boomerang* of Laramie, the Montana
Daily Rustler, the *Reese River Reveille*, the *Red
River Prospector*, the *Owyhee Avalanche*, and the
Fairplay Flume would be dull and stereotyped. Add
to them the voice of *The Territorial Enterprise*, with
Dan de Quille and Mark Twain on the staff, and the
shenanigans of the *Denver Post* under Bonfils and
Tammen, and the student of Western newspaper-
dom has a fistful to draw to.

The editors and reporters for the Western papers,
however, had a besetting problem which did not
exist in the big cities. There were, of course, vivid
items of shootings and knifings, murder trials, in-
quests, and big stories of mine accidents or political
scandals, but there were also blank periods and lulls
which could prove fatal to the paper and to the reporter who was not resourceful. Out of very necessity, then, the editors concocted the hoaxes which

were so characteristic of Western journalism. To fill
space, to entertain their readers, and to amuse themselves, they created stories which traveled around
the world, stories often believed completely by the
literal-minded and, for others, sources of high
amusement.

Not only did editors create stories, but they created whole communities in which to set their stories,
as well as purely fictitious newspapers with which
to fight. The *Carson Appeal* fought tooth and nail
with the nonexistent *Wabuska Mangler* over a
period of several years, and there are perhaps Westerners alive today who will swear that the *Mangler*
was one of the liveliest sheets ever published—simply on the basis of the *Appeal's* attacks. The *Appeal*
reprinted savage editorials credited to the *Mangler*
and called its editor a "disgrace to journalism."
When it grew tired of keeping the *Mangler* alive,
the *Appeal* killed off the editor by announcing that
he had skipped the country one jump ahead of the
sheriff.

Jim Townsend, who began his career with the
Mono Index in Mono County and wound it up in
Carson, populated his small town with ten thousand
inhabitants and kept them constantly in uproar.
One exciting episode was a shooting scrape and di-
vorce proceedings involving the Mayor, his wife,
and a member of the City Council. It made interesting reading and was implicitly believed—except by

those who knew that there was no mayor or council in town. Townsend enlivened his columns with killings, law suits, murder trials, railroad accidents, and a thousand and one incidents of daily life in a humming, growing city, every last one of which he coined out of his own active brain. He was a unique and versatile liar, and was known as Lying Jim to his death.

Fred Hart, who founded the Sazerac Lying Club and ran the *Reese River Reveille*, peppered his Austin readers with tall tales and hoaxes. And Major John Dennis, who printed the *Tuscarora Times Review*, recounted with utmost gravity his discovery of a "luminous shrub" that grew near Tuscarora. His account was seriously reprinted and discussed throughout the United States, and several Eastern botanists even came to Nevada to investigate it.

But chief of all hoaxsters was Dan de Quille, the greatest of the reporters for *The Territorial Enterprise*. His daily work was a model of accuracy, and his news accounts were implicitly believed. His reputation for dependability was such that all his readers who were unacquainted with his joking proclivity accepted as truth every word he wrote. This made De Quille's hoaxes all the more dangerous, particularly since he prepared them with scientific minuteness and presented them in a straightforward, reportorial style.

Best known were his two hoaxes about the

traveling stones of Pahranagat Valley and the
death of Jonathan Newhouse, inventor of the solar
armor. De Quille claimed that a prospector roaming through the wild Pahranagat Mountains of
southeastern Nevada had discovered a large number of round, heavy stones about the size of wal-
nuts. "When scattered about on the floor, within
two or three feet of each other, they immediately
began traveling toward a common center, and then
huddled up in a bunch like a lot of eggs in a nest."
The full story traveled around the world, and De
Quille was plagued and bedeviled for the next fifteen years answering letters about these stones.
Scientists in Germany accused him of a lack of
professional ethics when he refused further information about them. Barnum offered him $10,-
000 if he could make them perform. A gentleman
named Haines wanted a carload to sell, offering to
split the profit with Dan. At last, weary of the jest,
he retracted in the *Enterprise* on November 11,
1879: "We have stood this thing about fifteen
years, and it is becoming a little monotonous. We
are now growing old, and we want peace. We desire to throw up the sponge and acknowledge the
corn; therefore, we solemnly affirm that we never
saw or heard of any such diabolical cobbles as the
traveling stones of Pahranagat. If this candid con-
fession shall carry a pang to the heart of any true
believer, we shall be glad of it, as the true believers

have panged it to us, right and left, quite long enough."

Jonathan Newhouse, "a man of considerable inventive genius," constructed an apparatus to protect men from desert heat, the chief characteristic of which was an evaporating agent which saturated a special, tightly laced hood and jacket, thus producing any degree of cold desired as the sun drew off the moisture. Unfortunately for Newhouse, the mechanism went haywire and the inventor was found in Death Valley by an excited Indian, frozen to death with an icicle a foot long dangling from his nose. This tale likewise reached Europe and was published somewhat cautiously by the London *Daily Telegraph*: "We confess that, although the fate of Mr. Newhouse is related *au grand serieux*, we should require some additional confirmation before we unhesitatingly accept it. But everyone who has iced a bottle of wine by wrapping a wet cloth round it and putting it in a draught, must have noticed how great is the cold that evaporation of moisture produces."

Dan recounted the story of a wonderful hot spring located one mile out from Elko on the White Pine road, "the water of which, when properly seasoned with pepper and salt, cannot be distinguished from the best chicken soup." He placed "sugar-cured, fat, Salt Lake grasshoppers" on sale at the store of E. Feusier and Company, comparing them favorably in succulence to crab and shrimp. He located a hill of peculiar "ringing rocks and singing stones" near Pyramid Lake in the old Truckee Mining District. "These stones gave out a constant tinkling sound, and their myriads of tinklings blending together produced a musical murmur of considerable volume. The stones emitting these sounds were described as containing much iron, and some supposed that the musical tinklings were produced by magnetic action, while others thought that the whole drift of stones might be slowly working downhill, and that the sounds were caused by the attraction of the fragments composing the mass."

He discovered the rare Shoo Fly, a "monster insect inhabiting a shallow, slimy lake, situated fourteen miles northeast of Mud Lake. These flies are seen in large flocks about the lake and dive into the water, where they can remain on the bottom for an indefinite length of time, being supplied with air from a large bubble which forms about and incloses the head. The grub or larva from which the fly is hatched is of a deep green color and is some six inches in length by four inches in circumference. It is much esteemed by the Indians, who roast it in the ashes, when it looks not unlike a sweet potato. It also has a vegetable taste, perhaps from feeding upon the rushes, whereas the flies found at Mono Lake and greedily devoured by the

Paiutes living in the neighborhood have a strong fishy taste, as also have the ducks which fatten on them." There was much more, and a learned entomologist in San Francisco wrote Dan, giving him elaborate packing instructions and saying, "I presume them to be rather a hymenopteron (wasp or bee) than a depteron (two-winged insect). Corresponding with the Smithsonian and other Societies, I shall communicate your contribution without delay, and you shall have all the merit and acknowledgement." Dan published the entomologist's request in the columns of the paper and commented, "What the professor says may be true, but when we view the insect and consider its cuspidated tentacles and the scarabaeus formation of the thoracic pellicle, we are inclined to think it a genuine bug of the genus 'hum.' "

He described the eucalyptus as a fine, healthy animal on exhibition in the aquarium at Woodward's Gardens in San Francisco. "It is twelve feet long, covered with a thin, short, black fur on the back, and light brown on the belly and sides, with black, zebralike stripes. But the most extraordinary thing about the formation of the eucalyptus is that the spine terminates in a fork, each branch of which extends like a tail and is some five feet in length. The vertebral bones continue through these tails, which have on their outer sides a broad, falcated membrane, along the outer edge of which, on each tail or wing, are three strong hooks, similar to those seen on the wings of a bat. There are only two stout pectoral flippers, and no dorsal or ventral fins. The eucalyptus is of a gentle and docile disposition, and may be handled without any fear of treachery."

He established Ed Chapin of the Petaluma Mill, Gold Hill, and Rube Hobart, of the hardware firm of Doake, Hobart and Company, in the cremation business. "The charge for cremating an ordinary cadaver will be but $15. For mothers-in-law—and here is where the profit comes in—they charge $25, a price that any average son-in-law will cheerfully pay." He evolved the Smoke-ometer, a device which would obviate the need for cigars and matches yet would provide the purest smoke to lovers of the weed. From a central Smoke Works, pipes were to run to all houses and saloons. "In every house where the smoke is taken, there will be placed a meter, similar to a gas meter, but much more delicately constructed. When a man desires to take a smoke, he has not to go to the trouble of hunting up tobacco and filling his pipe, then of finding and lighting a match, and perhaps burning his fingers, and afterward getting fire and ashes upon his clothes half a dozen times before his smoke is ended. There is none of this trouble and vexation. He has only to place an amber mouthpiece between his lips, turn a small silver thumb-screw, and the cool, delicious, perfumed smoke glides into his mouth."

Still another hoax was endorsed as entirely feasible by a leading Eastern engineering journal. De Quille outlined the next thing to perpetual motion in pumping machinery by proposing that a windmill be constructed to hoist loose sand, in addition to the usual load of water, during the hours when the wind blew. When the wind died, the sand, by gravitation, would continue to operate turbine wheels and thus keep on pumping water. His description of the apparatus, which he said had been invented by Colonel James W. E. Townsend—Lying Jim—was so convincing that an engineer in Boston actually figured out the exact horsepower capable of being produced by the machinery.

Only slightly less believable were Mark Twain's Nevada hoaxes. Twain won his boots, spurs, and his whole writing equipment in the West. He had Dan de Quille beside him as colleague, reporter, and example of Western wit. Around him in the West were also men like Sam Davis, J. W. Gally, Fred Hart, J. Ross Browne, Jim Townsend, Jim Gillis, Rollin Dagget, and others. Joseph T. Goodman, editor of the *Enterprise*, encouraged him. Reminiscing later, Goodman said, "Isn't it so singular that Mark Twain should live and Dan de Quille fade out? If anyone had asked me in 1863 which was to be an immortal name, I should unhesitatingly have said Dan de Quille." Goodman's own explanation for the reversal of his estimate was that De Quille "shrank from the world, while Mark Twain braved it, and the world recognized his audacity." There was a certain element of *épater le bourgeois* in Twain's writings, a love of shock and satire, which was lacking in the gentleness of De Quille. De Quille's hoaxes were gentle; Twain's barbed. De Quille never would have concocted a gory murder as a vehicle for attack upon stock speculation, as Twain did.

On October 28, 1863, Twain's story of the Hopkins murders appeared in the *Enterprise* under the at once improbable headline: "A Victim to Jeremy Diddling Trustees—He Cuts his Throat from Ear to Ear, Scalps His Wife, and Dashes out the Brains of Six Helpless Children!" No one reading the hoax was concerned with improbabilities. No one bothered to remark that there was no "great pine forest" but only sagebrush between Empire City and Dutch Nick's. No one bothered to ask whether anyone knew the mythical family slaughtered by Twain. They read with horror and believed.

"It seems that during the past six months a man named P. Hopkins, or Philip Hopkins, has been residing with his family in the old log house just at the edge of the great pine forest which lies between Empire City and Dutch Nick's. The family consisted of 9 children—5 girls and 4 boys—the oldest of the group, Mary, being 19 years old, and the youngest, Tommy, about a year and a half. . . .

"About 10 o'clock on Monday evening, Hopkins dashed into Carson on horseback, with his throat cut from ear to ear, and bearing in his hand a reeking scalp from which the warm, smoking blood was still dripping, and fell in a dying condition in front of the Magnolia Saloon. Hopkins expired in the course of five minutes, without speaking. The long red hair of the scalp he bore marked it as that of Mrs. Hopkins. A number of citizens, headed by Sheriff Gasherie, mounted at once and rode down to Hopkins' house, where a ghastly scene met their gaze. The scalpless corpse of Mrs. Hopkins lay across the threshold, with her head split open and her right hand almost severed from the wrist. Near her lay the ax with which the murderous deed had been committed. In one of the bedrooms, six of the children were found, one in bed and the others scattered about the floor. They were all dead. Their brains had evidently been dashed out with a club, and every mark about them seemed to have been made with a blunt instrument. The children must have struggled hard for their lives, as articles of clothing and broken furniture were strewn about the room in utmost confusion. Julia and Emma, aged respectively 14 and 17, were found in the kitchen, bruised and insensible, but it is thought their recovery is possible. The eldest girl, Mary, must have sought refuge in her terror in the garret, as her body was found there frightfully mutilated, and the knife with which her wounds had been inflicted still sticking in her side."

Hopkins's derangement, which precipitated this carnage, was laid by Twain to the "cooking and watering" of stock. "We hope the fearful massacre detailed above may prove the saddest result of the silence of cunning financiers." In spite of a retraction—"I take it all back. Mark Twain."—published the following day, the uproar occasioned in town by the account was so great that Twain thought seriously of leaving the Comstock. Goodman, however, strongly supported him and he remained to continue writing.

Both Twain and Dan de Quille perpetrated hoaxes about petrified men, and the difference between the two writers is again apparent. De Quille detailed, with scientific exactness, the discovery of a body which, in a sealed mountain cavern, had been turned from that of a living Indian into a "silver man." The nature of the earth, steaming vapors, and the transfer of metallic substances to the body over a period of centuries had literally changed the body into a "mass of sulphuret of silver, slightly mixed with copper and iron." De Quille's knowledge of chemistry and mineralogy caused the account to be seriously accepted. Twain's petrified man, on the other hand, was seated on a hillside, "the right thumb resting against the side of the nose . . . and the fingers of the right hand spread apart."

. . . AND "BRONCO" LAZZERI

THAT the tradition of hoaxing is not altogether dead in the West was demonstrated with Peter Burke's willingness—news being scant—to publish in his *Virginia City News* an account by the present writer of the tragic demise of "Bronco" Lazzeri. Those who read and believed did not bother to remember that Bronco's full name was Frank Nello Lazzeri and that he and his "cousin" were one and the same; that Mr. Roger Butterfield was in Hart-

296

wick, New York; that Bronco's establishment had
no elegant plush furnishings and no deer head;
that his attitude toward coins of the realm was
highly possessive; and that his instinct for retaining
control of his stock of liquors—until cash lay on
the barrelhead—was well-developed. As was also
his sense of humor.

Some who read were delighted to know of Bronco's "death," and wrote letters to the *News* to that
effect. Others sorrowed, and sent flowers or checks
for flowers. Still others were mighty in their wrath
and, believing the truth of the "death," castigated
the reporter for indelicacies. There was general
chaos for a time, much howling from Los Angeles,
and a concerted drive to anchor deer heads firmly
to saloon walls.

Under the banner-head, "Tragic and Shocking
Death on Comstock," and with three subheads, "Beloved V. C. Philanthropist Passes Away," "Frank
'Bronco' Lazzeri Dies in Union Brewery," and "Depraved Actions of Tourists in Virginia City," the
story occupied the full front page of the paper in
its regular issue of June 26, 1948. Dispensing with
quotes:

It was a shocked and grief-stricken city that
learned yesterday of the sudden passing of "Bronco" Lazzeri, a death made the more tragic because
of the gruesome and heartrending manner of his
demise. The present writer. whose difficult task it

is to report the tragedy, had anticipated only his usual pleasant stay with friends on C Street during a short visit. But the sudden passing of an old friend makes imperative the writing of this obituary, a final tribute to a great character who enlivened the community during his declining years. It is with sadness that this is written, real personal grief, and yet there remains with the writer a feeling that somehow he was selected to be here at Mr. Lazzeri's end, so that the Comstock might know all the details of his death. With full reportorial accuracy in the face of his unbelievable and hideous death agony, and yet with a humility before the awfulness of the grave to which we must all come, this account is faithfully recorded for Comstock history. Mr. John Zalac's kind permission to use the second panguingui table at the Smokery Club for the purpose of writing this obit is gratefully acknowledged.

As all C Street habitués are aware, Mr. Lazzeri's elegant establishment is directly opposite Mr. Giraudo's grocery store on the east side of the street and only a few doors below the Bucket of Blood Saloon. It is, therefore, in an active part of town, in a spot where any untoward activity would quickly be noted. Yet—and we write this with horror— Mr. Lazzeri suffered the agonies of the damned for four full hours before friends found him in a desperate and hopeless condition. We can only ac-

count for this, ironically enough, through the generosity and *joie de vivre* which made Mr. Lazzeri
a favorite of the community. It was always his
custom to allow fun-loving members of the town
to gather at his bar, and their noise—while innocent and carefree—dominated the area. So that
when Mr. Lazzeri was himself stricken and cried
out with the pains of hell in his stomach, residents
assumed that no more than a normal "bout" was
in progress. Actually it was Bronco alone, thrashing from bar to spittoon to door—unfortunately
closed—to privy (also closed), to bar, to spittoon,
in what must have seemed to Mr. Lazzeri an endless eternity of frustrating activity. It is surprising
that he lived as long as he did. Mr. Robert Emmett
Berry, our District Attorney, who capably investi-
gated the reasons for death and who was himself
present at the last, commented that "in all my
experience there has been nothing like this on the
Comstock Lode."

It appears that Bronco's first fatal pangs were
felt at precisely 1:43 p.m. yesterday, Friday, June
25. At that moment, Mr. Roger Butterfield, well-
known historian and resident on the Lode, left Mr.
Lazzeri's palatial bar, unwittingly leaving behind
him the change from a five-dollar bill. As Mr. Butterfield passed the Silver Dollar Hotel he recol-
lected his money and immediately returned, "not
wasting a moment," according to testimony. Unac-

countably the money remained on the bar, but
there was no sign of Mr. Lazzeri. It would seem
that Mr. Lazzeri was stricken in the act of reaching
for Mr. Butterfield's change—to return it to him if
he could find him on the street—and had slumped
behind his rosewood bar. Mr. Butterfield, therefore, was in the presence of death as he picked up
his $4.50. How easily this could happen to all of us!

Mr. Butterfield signed an affidavit to the effect
that when he left Mr. Lazzeri's saloon he closed
the door behind him, since no one seemed to be in
the place. This affidavit is on file with the District
Attorney's office. Had Mr. Butterfield not closed
the door, Bronco might still be with us. But Mr.
Butterfield certainly cannot be held responsible in
any way under the circumstances.

The noise which Bronco made while struggling
in agony attracted no attention, as we have said,
for four hours. His agonized screams were interpreted by Comstock passers-by as simply boisterous
protests by Bronco to old-time customers, telling
them to put their money away and that drinks
were on the house. He disliked taking money from
friends, and when they offered payment for drinks
he could be heard protesting in his familiar and
well-loved voice for a city block.

No account was taken of the tragedy being en-
acted behind the fabulous cut-glass doors until Mr.
Edward Blake, known to us as "Deacon," saw a

trickle of blood running from under the left-hand door onto the wooden sidewalk. As an old news-paperman, "Deacon" had covered many saloon fights on the Comstock and was present at the famous murder when Sam Brown cut the heart of an innocent bystander and then calmly went to sleep on a billiard table. He was at once alert to what might be happening.

MR. BLAKE'S COMMENT

Springing to his feet, he rushed to the door and pushed it open. The sight which met his eyes is almost beyond belief. Deacon's own words describe his emotions: "It was the god-damndest thing I ever saw." We record his exact words somewhat hesitantly because Deacon, as his sobriquet indicates, is not given to profanity. We do not wish in these columns to give offense, and believe that we will be forgiven in quoting Deacon exactly because of the great emotional strain under which he spoke.

What met his gaze was horrible in the extreme. Stretching and writhing on the floor was the twitch-ing body of Mr. Lazzeri. His feet were extended toward the famous china spittoons at the left of the entrance, while his hands groped horribly for sup-port toward the rich plush benches at the right. With one hand Bronco had even clawed through the heavy Brussels carpet to dig at splinters in the timbered floor.

Resting upon Mr. Lazzeri's back was the great mounted deer head which had decorated his back bar. As visitors to his establishment will remember, this enormous stuffed head was Mr. Lazzeri's pride. He had shot it himself with one of the guns from his large collection, had it mounted at great expense, and—in the great Comstock tradition— had each of the ten points tipped in silver from his own mine. These points were resultingly extremely sharp. The head weighed, with its special mounting, exactly 197 pounds.

Without realizing that two points were imbedded in Mr. Lazzeri, Mr. Blake attempted to lift the head from his body. Mr. Lazzeri gave a prolonged and hideous groan and fainted away. Mr. Blake's efforts succeeded only in increasing the flow of blood, and in a brief space Mr. Lazzeri's body lay lifeless on the floor. In Mr. Blake's behalf it must be said that Bronco could not possibly have lived, and Mr. Blake's action actually placed him peacefully beyond agony which no man should suffer.

DREADFUL SHAMBLES

By this time many tourists had gathered, as well as Comstock residents from nearby stores and saloons. They were appalled at the shambles which the interior of the Union Brewery Saloon represented. Blood was literally one-fourth of an inch deep in the saloon, behind the bar, under the benches, and across the rare carpets. Lace curtains had been torn from the French windows, whisky bottles from the lower bar rolled on the floor, chairs were upturned—in short, literally everything within Mr. Lazzeri's reach, as he had crawled around the room, was upset or destroyed.

The peace officers of the Comstock were at once on hand and began to control the crowd, some of whom pushed forward simply out of morbid curiosity, while others sincerely wished to know the state of Mr. Lazzeri's condition.

We must note with shocked indignation that certain tourists, who were later observed to depart in a car with California license plates, had the bad taste and terrible effrontery to dip poker chips in the blood which oozed out onto the sidewalk. Their actions were noted by Mr. Tex Gladding and Mr. Pat Hart, who at once gave them a good Nevada heave-ho of which they can be justifiably proud.

Conjecturally reconstructed, the tragedy appears to have taken place in this form. Mr. Butterfield was known to have been drinking milk highballs at the Union Bar. Mr. Lazzeri himself, as all the Comstock knows, never touched milk, but he had the frugal habit—and one which contributed to his wealth—of saving the remains of all drinks. Those which were palatable he tended to finish himself, and those which were not he pooled in a common receptacle, reselling to Los Angeles tourists under the amusing name of "Bug Juice."

The remains of Mr. Butterfield's milk highball, however, he would not drink himself nor could he mix with the "Bug Juice"—naturally amber in color—since it would produce a drink somewhat the color of lye, to which even a Los Angeles tourist might reasonably object.

Bronco, therefore, took the remnants of Mr. Roger Butterfield's drink, poured it into a small shot glass and placed it in the refrigerator. As he did so, he caught sight of Mr. Butterfield's $4.50 change on the bar. Instead, then, of carefully shutting the icebox door—directly under the buck head —he turned quickly back to the bar to retrieve Mr. Butterfield's money (to return to him) and gave a quick back kick to the icebox door. This kick was delivered with such force that the buck head was loosened from its hangings and fell down upon Bronco just as he was stretched forward, his back vulnerable to any blow. The terrific force with which the buck's head hit may be judged by the fact that the two silver-tipped points penetrated Bronco's posterior abdominal region to a depth of six and seven inches, respectively.

Just at the moment of the blow, it would seem, while Mr. Lazzeri lay momentarily stunned, Mr. Butterfield entered for his change. Had Mr. Butterfield waited only a few moments, instead of hastily retrieving his $4.50, he might again have saved Bronco's life.

HORRIBLE AGONY

As it was, Bronco recovered himself slightly after Mr. Butterfield's departure and began his agonizing and tortuous circuit of his saloon, crawling for aid which never came and crying aloud for assistance which was denied him. The pain must have been excruciating and we do not like to dwell upon it. We only ask the reader to place himself in Mr. Lazzeri's position, to feel two terrific holes over the kidneys topped by a weight of 197 pounds, and then to picture himself slithering around the floor in his own blood, screaming in torments which Dante never dreamed of.

And all this time Mr. Blake was sitting within ten feet of the Union Brewery doors, calmly sunning himself and dreaming of the old Comstock days.

The ways of life and the manners of death are things upon which we should all ponder.

Mr. Lazzeri's demise occurred at exactly 5:42 P.M. when Mr. Blake pulled the horns out of his back, and it was not long before news of the terrible tragedy had reached the whole Comstock and been telephoned by Mrs. Edna James to Dayton, Carson City, and Reno, where Mr. Lazzeri had numerous friends.

FUNERAL PLANS

Plans were at once made on the Comstock to inter the body with the dignity which his past life demanded. The first billiard table of the Smokery Saloon was decorated with hastily picked flowers from McDevitt's Gardens and the body was respectfully laid upon it after the billiard balls had been racked by Eddie Colletti.

The Comstock, always ready with its committees, quickly created a new one composed of leading citizens to arrange for the funeral. It was decided that the cortege would depart from the Fire House at 3:00 P.M. on Wednesday, June 30. Many residents have volunteered their cars to form the funeral procession, and those who do not have rides may obtain them by registering with Mr. William Marks at the Original Crystal Bar. Cars will be parked on side streets between C and B, but before an individual may ride he must obtain his car assignment from Mr. Marks.

Mr. Carl Boegle, Chief of Police, will be in charge of directing traffic and it is anticipated that tourists coming from Carson will be deflected to B Street from the Divide. Tourists coming from Reno will be halted beyond the Sierra Nevada works until the cortege passes down C Street from the Fire House to the Six Mile Canyon road. Descending Six Mile a short distance, the procession will follow

the Hospital Road past the City Dumps, the Arizona-
Comstock Tailings, and take the old road to the
Flowery Hill Cemetery, a place hallowed in the
memory of all Comstockers and where many great
figures of our past, including Julie Bullette, are
buried. The road to this hallowed ground has recently been made passable by Louis Siegriest a well-
known artist on the Comstock. Sand had drifted
over a part of it and he did some honest work for
the Comstock when he shoveled it away.

Mr. George Ingram, a recent arrival on the Comstock and popular proprietor of the Virginia Club
Saloon, is a member of the Lazzeri Funeral Committee. Mr. Ingram has enlivened the Comstock
with his Tuesday-night dances and he has come
forth with a suggestion which all proprietors of C
Street establishments should consider seriously.
Namely, that all establishments owning juke boxes
play the "Beer Barrel Polka" as the cortege departs
from the Fire House. This was known to be a favorite tune of Mr. Lazzeri and we feel that he would
appreciate this spontaneous homage to his memory. Proprietors playing the tune should leave their
doors open so that C Street may really resound.

As the cortege passes beyond the sounds of the
"Polka," it has been proposed that the Fire House
siren attempt to play "Nearer My God to Thee,"
a hymn which Mr. Lazzeri is also known to have
loved. This will be heard on the Hospital Road.

ONE-GUN SALUTE

Passing the Hospital itself, Mr. John Bowie will fire a one-gun salute. Mr. Bowie proposed this himself and stated that the powder was saved from blasting some two years ago at the Con-Virginia works where Mr. Zeb Kendall, prominent Comstock mining man, has been active. Mr. Bowie, who is in charge of the Hospital grounds and is the first surviving white child to be born on the Comstock, pointed out that this would not be at the expense of the County. It is a personal tribute from himself.

He is to be congratulated.

Beyond the Hospital, the cortege will proceed with the solemnity which the occasion deserves and there will be no additional music, even of a lugubrious and inspiring nature.

The scene at Flowery Hill we will leave to the profound imagination of our readers. Those who have visited this isolated yet beautiful spot will always retain a feeling of mystic majesty. The Washoe zephyr blows gently through small firs and desert flowers bloom there in delicate tribute to those who have passed on.

STOMACH FOR NEVADA

Reportorially, it should be noted that not all of Mr. Lazzeri will be buried at Flowery Hill. When news of his death reached Carson City, one of the

Directors of the State Museum, Mr. William Donovan of nearby Silver City, immediately hurried to
the Comstock and proposed that Mr. Lazzeri's stomach be deposited with the permanent state collection.

Comstockers will remember that Mr. Lazzeri,
apart from his affectionate nickname of "Bronco,"
was also known as "Iron Stomach." Many of us remember the fantastic concoctions which he poured
down, including, most recently, hot coffee mixed
equally with fruit juice and a dash of tabasco. No
one on the Comstock denies the strength of his stomach. He drank wine, beer, whisky, gin, all known
liqueurs, soda pop, and everything liquid except
milk until the last. He could pour wine in beer, gin
in whisky, and drink any combination of liquors
without a qualm.

He ate like a horse, and smoked like a chimney.
All of us will remember the friendly trays of food
carried with such care by Florence Ballou Edwards,
genial hostess of the Silver Dollar, to him as he
worked quietly building his Virginia City affairs.
Mr. Glenn Harris reported seven trays in one day,
each one loaded with delicacies. But to top the
trays, Mr. Lazzeri also ate gallon cans of fruit,
pickles, jars of hot peppers, pig's feet, whole onions,
strings of hot sausage, salami, and virtually anything edible within reach.

The fame of his stomach was not merely a local

matter. Tourists had carried word of it throughout the country, and even the Smithsonian Institution in Washington and the Museum of Natural History in New York were aware of it. Word of it also reached the Musée de l'Homme in Paris. It is therefore greatly to the credit of the Carson City Museum, and the instant activity of Mr. William Donovan, that Mr. Lazzeri's intestines were acquired intact for Nevada. Had there been any delay in the matter, Nevada would have been the loser.

MOUNTED IN LUCITE

The intestines have been mounted in plastic lucite and placed upon a revolving turntable so that the scientist, as well as visitors from California, may view them from all angles at their leisure. Comstockers will regret that they are not an attraction on the Lode, but should be pleased, nevertheless, in the knowledge that Mr. Lazzeri's stomach is the first Nevada stomach—and perhaps the first stomach west of the Rockies—to be preserved in this new translucent material.

Residents of the Comstock will be glad to learn that Mr. Lazzeri's philanthropy, normal to him in everyday life, extended beyond death. We are not acquainted with the full contents of his will, but do know this much—that he left a certain sum, said to be in the neighborhood of $1000, distributed equally among the eighteen bars on C Street. This fund is to be used within two days of the funeral, and each bar is to distribute drinks gratis to resident Comstockers who will naturally wish to drink to Mr. Lazzeri and his generosity. Tourists may not participate. In view of their ghoulish blood-dipping of poker chips, Mr. Lazzeri exercised wise judgment.

In addition, Mr. Lazzeri specified that within two days of his death all liquid stock in his establishment was to be consumed by his regular customers. Such customers should avail themselves of this opportunity at once, since the two-day time limit will close tomorrow at 5:42 P.M., at which time the remaining stock will revert to the estate, now being handled by the County until heirs have time to appear.

Regular customers visiting the Union Brewery now may be surprised to find a Mr. Lazzeri, a cousin of our own Mr. Lazzeri, tending bar. His first name, however, is Nello and not Frank. In appearance he resembles Bronco, but we regret to note that in temperament he does not come up to our old friend, tending to growl at customers and to grab at every penny. This was not like Mr. Frank Lazzeri and the contrast is the more striking in view of Broncos' recent presence among us, genial, cordial, friendly, generous. We regret the necessity of mentioning this but do believe that truth should prevail on the Comstock.

Lack of space in the present issue forbids our discussion of Mr. Lazzeri's birth, his youthful upbringing, his early education, his financial struggles in Chicago and the East, and his arrival on the Comstock, attended by subsequent success. We shall report this in our next issue together with a detailed account of the funeral, which will undoubtedly be one of the most elaborate held on the Comstock.

PALLBEARERS

Pallbearers at the funeral will be Mr. Edward Blake, Mr. James Whiteside, Mr. Charles Addis, Mr. Jack Colford, Mr. John Harrington, and "Four Day" Jack Sunara.

Honorary pallbearers will include Mr. Zeb Kendall, Mr. William Curran, Senator Mervyn Gallagher, Mr. Al Spargo, Mr. Al Jacobson, and Mr. John Kelly.

Chief mourner will be Mr. Jack Tessadio.

It is greatly regretted by the present writer that he will not be on the Comstock at the time of the funeral to pay final homage to a great pioneer. It is equally regretted that Mr. Lazzeri's largesse, distributed through the eighteen bars, will pass the writer by.

However, we shall all be together in spirit, and no distance can separate us or those who loved Mr. Lazzeri. Our thoughts will all be with him as he rests on Flowery Hill, his gentle and great presence brooding over C Street and the Union Brewery.

Farewell, kind friend!

Note: Flowers should be sent to the Silver Dollar Hotel to arrive not later than twelve noon, June 30.